Techniques of a Professional Commodity Chart Analyst

Techniques of a Professional Commodity Chart Analyst

Arthur Sklarew

E P B M

ECHO POINT BOOKS & MEDIA, LLC
Brattleboro, Vermont

Published by Echo Point Books & Media
Brattleboro, Vermont
www.EchoPointBooks.com

Techniques of a Professional Commodity Chart Analyst
ISBN: 978-1-64837-409-8 (casebound)
978-1-64837-410-4 (paperback)

Cover design by Kaitlyn Whitaker

To my wife, Jeanette,
who lovingly shares me
with my commodity charts.

Acknowledgments

I was fortunate to have as my publisher a firm with specialized knowledge in the field of commodity research and price analysis. I am indebted to its president, William L. Jiler, to their senior editor, Walter Emery, and to their staff of chart technicians for the long hours they spent studying the manuscript and for their critical review of the text.

Special thanks is due to Todd Lofton for his editorial assistance, to Seymour Gaylinn and his art staff for their help in preparing the numerous charts, and to Irv Schnider for his attention to the many details in preparation for publication.

Much of my research into the nature of commodity price movements was inspired by the questions and comments of friends and clients whose commodity orders I handled over the years. Acknowledgment is due for their part in making this book possible.

Arthur Sklarew

Preface

As some of my associates know, this book was a long time in the writing. The study of commodity price chart analysis is so vast and the possible variations of most techniques are so numerous, that much time was consumed with additional research in the course of the writing.

Before including a recommendation of any technique that I had found to be effective in the past, I explored many alternate possibilities. To avoid burdening the reader with lengthy studies of each technical aspect covered, I have tried to keep the text as brief as possible, and have emphasized the techniques that I consider most valuable and the variations that I believe to be most helpful.

Most of the work in this book is original, based on concepts that I developed over the years; the balance covers techniques already known, some of which I have expanded or varied.

This book is directed primarily to commodity traders who have already been working with commodity price charts, or who are at least familiar with the well-known elementary techniques. It is also assumed that the reader needs no introduction to the commodity futures markets or to the functions of the various commodity exchanges.

The purpose of technical analysis, of course, is to anticipate the future direction of prices. I hope the techniques described in this book will prove helpful to the reader and enable him to benefit financially from a better forecasting ability.

A. S.

Foreword

Commodity futures trading has changed dramatically in the past decade. Ten years ago the cost of the most rudimentary computer was a quarter of a million dollars, and the few people who knew how to talk to it were considered gurus. The application of computers to futures trading was even more esoteric.

Today the click-buzz of computers almost drowns out the shouting in the pits in Chicago and New York.

What has been lost in the transition is that which is always lost when handcraft yields to automation. The profits are still there. In fact, if we can believe the proponents of mechanized trading their profits are greater than ever. What is lost is the "art" of technical analysis, the personal satisfaction of producing good results with one's own hand. Commodities, unlike common stocks, are a zero-sum game. What you gain, someone else must lose. It's one thing when your money manager's computer outwits the other players. It's quite another when *you* do.

The computer's approach to the markets is necessarily technical. Its grist is quantitative: prices, trading volume, and open interest. The hand-held counterpart is the daily-action price chart, showing high, low, and closing prices for each day (and, often, charted daily trading volume and open interest). The price chart has been the principal working tool of market technical analysts since the first futures contract was traded in Chicago more than 100 years ago.

This is a book for the chartist. For someone who believes, like any cryptographer, that hidden somewhere in those inky marks is an intelligible message.

It's a book for the commodity trader who enjoys the game itself. Who likes to call most of the plays, based on his own assessment of the market. Who takes almost as much satisfaction in being right as he does in the dollars it adds to his equity.

There's no hard-core *technicalia* here. The closest the author gets to electronic data processing is to suggest that some of the calculations would lend themselves well to manipulation by a hand-held calculator. There *is* a lacing of market lore, of insight based on observations probably long since relegated to the author's subconscious, like the old sea captain who can sniff the wind and tell you what tomorrow's weather will be.

There is also plenty of practical trading methodology, the use of which will be delimited only by the amount of time you want to spend working with charts and prices. Some of the ground the author covers is familiar. But most of it is not. His "Rule of Seven" and "17-35 Measurement," for examples, are innovative and, in my opinion, particularly useful for estimating price objectives.

Nothing the author presents, of course, is warranted against failure. There are always people running around the fringes of the commodity markets shouting, "I've got the secret." Arthur Sklarew is not among them. The trading strategies he offers are not formulae for sudden riches. They are objective guides to a more reasoned approach to trading decisions and each trader will be able to utilize them in his own way to improve his chance of success in the market.

Perhaps even more important than the specific trading methods is the trading philosophy with which the book is imbued. The author counsels cool patience. Whether it be a home, a car, 5,000 bushels of December wheat, buying or selling impulsively is rarely advantageous. But if you wait, you must have something to wait for. In the futures markets, technical analysis provides that something. Technical analysis gives you a rationale for selecting from the entire universe of prices one particular price level as the place to take action. By giving you a basis for selecting the "cut" point, it provides the kind of external discipline necessary to help you convert "cutting your losses short and letting your profits run" from an ideal into a feasible trading goal.

Since you have this book in your hands, I must assume that you are either into chart analysis or want to be. Fair enough. The author takes for granted that you know *something* about price charts. But even if you are new to the subject, there is little here that you won't understand and be able to apply. In fact, almost every trading strategy presented can be followed by you at home with nothing more than scratch paper, pencil, price charts, and the quotes from your daily newspaper.

If that sounds like it might be fun, start reading.

Todd Lofton

Contents

CHAPTER **1**

Some Basic Concepts

What Commodity Price Chart Analysis is all About

If there is one word that best describes what commodity price chart analysis is all about, that word is "TREND." Commodity futures traders, whether "local" pit traders, speculators, or commercial hedgers, all hope to profit by riding a trend—be it a price move lasting an hour, a day, a month, or a year. The purpose of commodity price chart analysis is to identify and evaluate price trends, with the objective of profiting from the future movement of prices. A chartist's asset lies not so much in his being able to forecast how *high* or how *low* a market will go, or *when* it will get there, as in being able to identify the *direction* of a trend and to call the *turn* of a trend when it comes. Most of the chart techniques described in this book have as their purpose the identification of trend direction.

Some commodity chart technicians have a preference for point-and-figure charts. Others prefer to concentrate on bar charts (showing daily high, low, and close). Many make use of both. Of those who watch bar charts, some prefer to use a logarithmic or a square-root price scale; but most find that the conventional arithmetic price scale serves them well. *The techniques described in these pages are intended for use primarily with bar charts using the conventional arithmetic scale.* Point-and-figure chart techniques will not be discussed, although some of the bar-chart techniques described here are also applicable to point-and-figure charts.

A Commodity Chartist Must Work at His Trading

Commodity trading is not an easy game. I think every trader would agree on that. There are times when it seems you can do no wrong; the market acts exactly as you expect it to act and the profits accumulate. And there are other times when almost every swing of the market gives you a frustrating loss.

It can be said with certainty that there is no perfect "method" for trading commodities; that is, one that will yield a profit on every trade. But there are many techniques and trading methods that can improve the odds of success. No one can pretend to have all the answers, but the trader who has a good working knowledge of chart techniques is at an advantage over the trader who has not made a study of market action.

A commodity chart technician must work hard at his market analysis. His charts must be updated daily and studied carefully for the proper application of his trend techniques. The techniques used must be selected with care, on the basis of his judgment of their past performance. His technical analysis must enable him to contend with market uncertainties caused by such things as unforeseen crop developments, weather, politics, and countless other forces that affect supply and demand. He must also compete with other sophisticated traders who are all trying their utmost to outsmart the market and each other.

There are two basic approaches to the analysis of commodity price trends. One is fundamental analysis, based on all the known factors that could affect the supply or demand of the commodity; the other is technical analysis, based entirely on an interpretation of the market action itself. This book deals solely with technical analysis.

Two Aspects of Commodity Chart Analysis

It may be helpful to view commodity chart analysis as consisting of two separate categories: (1) general price chart techniques; and,

(2) automatic trading techniques. The general chart techniques include the interpretation of chart formations, seasonal tendencies, cyclical swings, trendlines, trend channels, measurement rules, and volume and open interest. Automatic trading methods, of which there are countless variations, include techniques that utilize minor and major trend swings, moving averages, oscillators, mechanical trendlines, and day-to-day price-range relationships. Volume and open interest could also be included in this category.

Both types of technical analysis are based solely on market action, without consideration of fundamental market forces. An important difference between the two technical approaches is the need for judgment when applying general price chart techniques. Interpretation of chart formations and other technical data, not being an exact science, is necessarily subjective; the action taken on the basis of the same data might vary from one trader to another. Automatic trading methods (when followed with discipline) eliminate almost all need for judgment, as they call for definite and specific action to be taken when signaled. Which of the two paths a chart trader follows will depend on his individual temperament and preferences.

The Rule of Multiple Techniques

Technicians know very well that price chart analysis is not an exact science. No single chart technique yet discovered is infallible. Despite this lack of perfection, price chart analysis can very often give reliable forecasts of trend direction.

One way of improving the reliability of a price forecast based on a chart signal is to require confirmation of that signal in other active contracts of that same commodity before accepting the signal as valid. A "buy" or "sell" signal given in one contract month, if not confirmed in other delivery months of that commodity, is likely to prove false. In his booklet, "How Charts Are Used in Commodity Price Forecasting," William L. Jiler says:

"The constant process of confirming each chart formation as it evolves cannot be stressed too positively. Confirmation is accomplished by comparing as many charts that are related to the commodity being analyzed as possible. For example, when attempting to determine whether a head and shoulders is developing in March Wheat, every other wheat contract should be studied for confirmation. The weekly and monthly continuation charts should always be consulted as well to affirm the longer range trend. . . . It is not at all uncommon to observe an almost perfect picture develop in one contract while an entirely different form takes shape in another delivery of the same commodity. Its subsequent move usually invites confusion. As a rule of thumb, regard all formations suspiciously when a majority of all charts examined fail to confirm, unless fundamental factors suggest that there should be a divergence. Also, the more complete the confirmation, the more dependable may be the predicted trend."[1]

Confirmation is therefore an essential component of every valid chart signal. In addition to comparing price charts of different contract months and time scales, it has been my experience that *the accuracy of any technical price forecast can be improved greatly by the application of a principle that I call the "Rule of Multiple Techniques."*

The Rule of Multiple Techniques requires that the chart technician not rely solely on one single technical signal or indicator, but look for confirmation from other technical indicators. The more technical indicators that confirm each other, the better the chance of an accurate forecast. The logic behind this rule is that if individual time-proven techniques tend to be right *most* of the time, a combination of several such techniques that confirm each other will tend to be right even more frequently.

There are various ways in which chart techniques can confirm each other. In Chapter 5, for example, several methods of projecting upside and downside objectives are described. When two or more such measurements cluster around the same general price level on a particular price chart, the probability of that target being reached is greatly enhanced.

A combination of trend lines, resistance levels, and measured objectives all telling the same story is especially likely to give a correct

[1] William L. Jiler, "How Charts Are Used in Commodity Price Forecasting," Commodity Research Publications Co., New York, 1977, p. 9.

forecast. For example, suppose that, following a prolonged price decline, the upside penetration of a downtrend line coincides with an upside penetration of a previous rally high just after a long-awaited downside objective has been achieved. The combination of the three constructive developments increases the likelihood that a bottom has been made, and that an uptrend is beginning.

An additional factor that might be given weight is the insight of the experienced trader, based on his own personal recollections. In the course of time, a commodity chart analyst lives through many different market situations, and sometimes can make use of a sort of "sixth sense" in the evaluation of his technical signals. A strong "feeling" about the chart pattern, *if based on a chartist's past experience with similar market action,* may be worth rating as one of the important ingredients in a combination of technical indicators. Some of this "feeling" might even be based on an awareness of important fundamental forces. Care must be taken, however, to avoid being influenced by one's current position in the market, and to avoid making a trading decision based on this "sixth sense" alone, without other supporting indicators.

The Principle of Selective Techniques

It may appear at first sight that the "Principle of Selective Techniques," because of its very title, must be in direct conflict with the Rule of Multiple Techniques. Such is not the case. The Rule of Multiple Techniques applies to the broad field of general chart analysis, while the Principle of Selective Techniques applies to automatic trading methods. In very general terms, the Principle of Selective Techniques states simply that the automatic trading method that appears to work better than other methods in a particular market at a particular time is the one that should be used in that market at that time. While the method selected will be based on hindsight, it will almost certainly be found to have foresight as well.

Before explaining this concept in detail, it should be pointed out that many experienced and knowledgeable chartists believe—and with good reason—that any chart technique worthy of consideration should be able to prove its effectiveness in many commodities over many years. There is no disputing this belief. All the classic chart formations and chart techniques that have earned a reputation for effectiveness have proved themselves over time, while special or unique techniques that appear to work like magic on occasion often fail when tested over a prolonged period.

I believe a fine distinction must be drawn between techniques used in chart analysis and techniques used in automatic trading methods. The rules that are applicable to chart analysis are not the same as those applicable to automatic trading methods. Chart analysis entails considerable personal judgment, but it must be based on time-tested techniques applied in accordance with the Rule of Multiple Techniques. Automatic trading techniques are applied mechanically and will be found to work best when used selectively in accordance with the Principle of Selective Techniques.

The tendency for commodity markets to differ in their characteristic price movements is described by William L. Jiler:

"One of the most significant and intriguing concepts derived from intensive chart studies by this writer is that of characterization, or habit. Generally speaking, charts of the same commodity tend to have similar pattern sequences which may be different from those of another commodity. In other words, charts of one particular commodity may appear to have an identity or a character peculiar to that commodity. For example, cotton charts display many round tops and bottoms, and even a series of these constructions, which are seldom observed in soybeans or wheat. The examination of soybeans charts over the years reveals that triangles are especially favored. Head and Shoulders formations abound throughout the wheat charts. All commodities seem to favor certain behavior patterns."[2]

It is apparent that there must be great differences in the forces of supply and demand affecting markets so vastly different as coffee, wheat, live cattle, silver, plywood, and treasury bills, to cite just a few. Coffee trees that have been destroyed as a result of frost cannot be quickly replaced; new plantings do not bear fruit for the first few years. A wheat crop that fails can usually be fully replanted for har-

[2] *Ibid.,* p. 8.

vest the following year. Price trends in plywood and lumber are influenced greatly by changes in the demand for new residential
housing, a factor that has absolutely no bearing on the trends of
most other commodities. Each commodity is dominated by its own
individual supply/demand factors, and trend-following techniques
are likely to be most effective when hand-tailored to fit the individual commodity.

The Principle of Selective Techniques requires first of all that the
automatic trend trader have at his disposal an "inventory" of several
alternative automatic trading methods, each of which he believes has
merit. Secondly, it is necessary to test those methods in the commodity to be traded by "paper-trading" it back at least a few months,
preferably in the maturing or nearby delivery contract. This procedure is based on the assumption (which I believe to be valid) that
any good trend-following method or automatic trading method that
has worked well in a maturing contract of a commodity is also likely
to work well for an extended period of time in the later contract
months. (An exception might be a maturing contract that ends a
crop year.)

After comparing the record of gains and losses by each method
tested, it will usually be obvious which method would have worked
best, and that method is the one that should be selected for that particular commodity. It is possible that the method selected in this
manner for a particular commodity might give consistently good results for many successive years. However, if the character of the market should appear to be changing, it might then be wise to run a
new series of tests.

The Principle of Selective Techniques is especially applicable in
the case of a trader who is concentrating his attention on perhaps
two or three specific commodities, and is specializing in those markets. The automatic trend trader who is "spread across the board"
may find it impractical to vary his trading system with each commodity, and of necessity might have to settle for a trading system
that he has found to be generally effective in most markets. He
could, of course, eliminate those commodities that have repeatedly
shown poor performance under his trading method.

There are numerous good trading methods that can be developed and utilized. Some examples of trend-following methods are included in the later chapters.

Charts Versus Fundamentals

The fact that only the technical approach is discussed in these pages is not an indication of this writer's disapproval of the fundamental approach. On the contrary, I believe that a chart technician should always be aware of the fundamentals that affect the commodities of interest to him.

Knowledgeable analysis of the supply of and demand for a commodity usually requires an intensive and continuous study of that commodity. In some commodities, demand is relatively stable and supply is the thing to watch. In other commodities, supply is a relatively stable factor and demand the big variable. The delicate balance of supply and demand can be upset by many factors, including economic trends, political events, labor strikes, international developments, extreme weather conditions, and natural calamities. There may sometimes be just one important fundamental factor—perhaps relatively obscure—that holds the key to the future direction of a market. The fundamental analyst who can pinpoint that key item and interpret it correctly at an early stage will be able to forecast more accurately the future course of prices in that commodity. Although a chart technician may tend to lean more on his charts than on fundamentals, he must not turn a deaf ear to fundamental analysis.

Fundamentals that sharply contradict major chart signals may serve as a warning of a possible false or premature signal, or of a short-lived price move ahead. And, of course, major statistical reports related to the supply or demand of a commodity, issued by government agencies or by authoritative private sources, can often have an immediate and dramatic effect on the movement of prices.

Nevertheless, there are knowledgeable chartists who *do* successfully ignore the fundamentals, especially if they are utilizing an automatic or computer-based trend-following method. Even then, some

awareness of changing market fundamentals can be helpful in determining *which* markets to select for good potential price movement
and which to ignore temporarily.

Although technical and fundamental analysis are vastly different
in their approaches to the market, there is one characteristic they
share: *each uses past data to project estimates of the future.* While both
types of analysis can yield highly accurate forecasts in the hands of an
expert, neither is infallible. Both charts and fundamentals can tell
you with certainty where you have been, but cannot be quite that
certain about where you are going. *Any forecast of the future must always be a projection based on data of the past.*

Commercial hedgers, who must live with the daily realities of
supply and demand in the cash market, naturally tend to lean heavily
on the familiar fundamentals. Nevertheless, many of them find that
a knowledge of technical analysis is valuable as an aid in the *timing* of
their hedge transactions. The individual who is responsible for placing the hedge orders to buy or sell for his firm is "on the spot" so to
speak. While in theory his hedge is simply a form of price insurance
whereby a loss in the futures market may be fully justified by an offsetting gain he makes in the cash market, the hedge trader who consistently loses for his firm in the futures market may find his job in
jeopardy. Even though some of his firm's profitable cash market
transactions may have been possible only because an offsetting hedge
position was taken in the futures market (thus enabling the firm to
do business it would not otherwise have done), the corporate offi-
cers might still take a dim view of losses in the futures market. It is
therefore mandatory for a hedge trader to try to operate in the futures market in the most profitable manner possible. This can be fa-
cilitated by using technical analysis for timing trades, with due
respect paid to trend direction.

Trends Versus Random Walk

In recent years the Random Walk theory of price movement has
received an increasing amount of attention. The basic tenets of this

theory are that individual price movements are random, and that past market action has no effect on future market action. Price chart analysis, on the other hand, is based on the theory that prices tend to move in trends, and that past price behavior can give clues to the future direction of the trend. Let us examine the merits of both theories.

Most randomness studies have focused on securities prices, and so their conclusions do not necessarily apply to commodity futures, which differ from securities in several important respects. Among the most important differences are: (1) Futures contracts have a limited lifetime; (2) Futures trading is a zero-sum game, in that there is a short position for every long position; and (3) Futures prices are tied to the cash prices of their underlying items, and these cash prices often change in ways that are clearly non-random (e.g., rallies from seasonal harvest lows). Whether futures anticipate cash market prices in such a way that their fluctuations are random is a question that will doubtless receive much more study in the years ahead.

The most thorough recent investigation into the randomness issue was done by the USDA in 1976. Jitendar S. Mann and Richard G. Heifner of the USDA examined 574 different futures contracts using a variety of statistical techniques, and concluded that "The results . . . provide substantial evidence that daily changes in commodity futures prices do not follow the normal (Gaussian) probability distribution. More importantly, these prices are not serially independent. . . ."[3] It is interesting to note that the most prominent deviation from randomness found was a tendency toward more very large or very small daily price fluctuations than chance alone would dictate. This is at least intuitively consistent with the widespread assumption that futures are characterized by persistent trends.

It is amusing and perhaps a bit sobering to realize that even wholly random price changes can produce chart patterns that look very much like those resulting from our real-life markets. Consider, for example, figs. 1 and 2. These charts are the result of two experiments conducted by the author. In the first experiment, 102 small

[3] Jitendar S. Mann and Richard G. Heifner, "The Distribution of Shortrun Commodity Price Movements," Economics Research Service, U.S.D.A., Washington, D.C., 1976, p. 16.

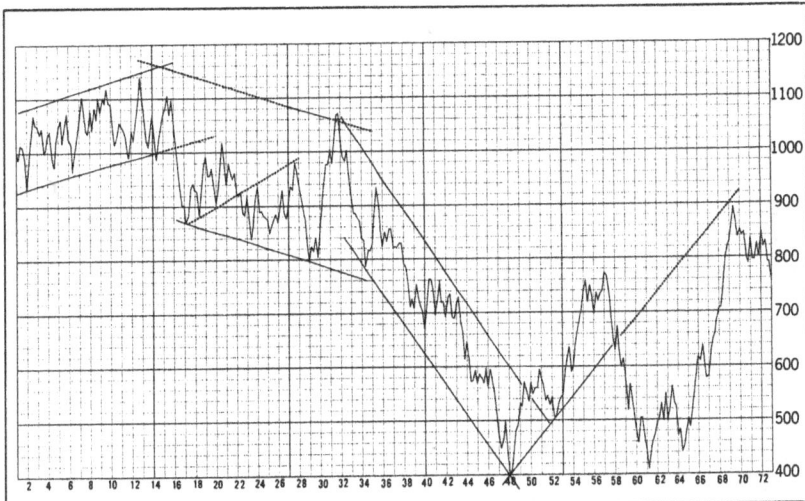

Figure 1. Random Walk: Random numbers from plus 50 to minus 50 representing net changes in daily closing prices (starting with a "price" of 1,000) generated this familiar-looking price chart, complete with major and minor "trend" lines.

squares of cardboard were prepared and numbered consecutively from zero to plus 50 and from zero to minus 50. The 102 pieces were then shaken thoroughly in a container, and one number was withdrawn blind. After recording the first number (which happened to be -12) it was thrown back, and the container was again shaken before drawing the second number ($+29$). This procedure was repeated for a total of 360 random drawings, each recorded in turn. To convert this list of "net changes" to a list of simulated daily closing prices, a nominal starting price of "1,000" was chosen and the plus and minus figures were added or subtracted in succession.

In the second experiment, 66 pieces were prepared, *three of each* from zero to plus 10 and from zero to minus 10. The same procedure of random drawing was then followed, except that *three* pieces were drawn each time. These were used to represent the "daily" net change of the high, low, and closing prices. The starting price used for this test was 100. A tabulation of the numbers drawn and their conversions to simulated prices appears in Appendix A.

It is interesting to note that although the numbers drawn at ran-

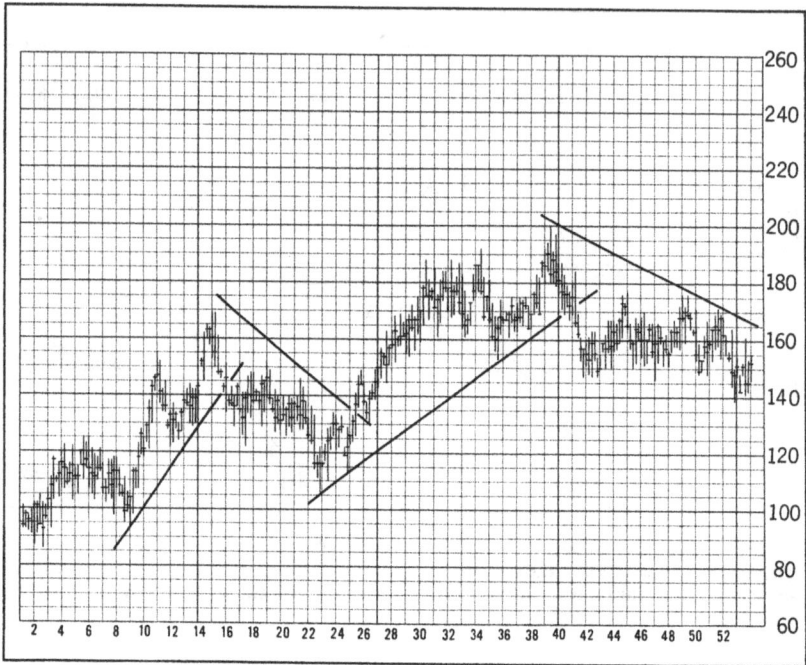

Figure 2. Random Walk: Simulated daily changes in high, low, and closing prices from plus 10 to minus 10 were selected at random to create this chart. As in Figure 1, "trend"-like behavior can be observed.

dom showed a wide disparity, and eventually carried the simulated price either far below or far above the starting point, the actual ratio of plus and minus values was closely in balance at the finish. Of the 360 numbers drawn in the first experiment, there were 171 pluses, 181 minuses, and 8 zeros. In the second experiment, out of 265 closing price changes there were 118 pluses, 115 minuses, and 32 zeros.

It is probable that similar experiments by the reader would yield different chart pictures, but *there seems little doubt that "trends" would be apparent in any reasonably extended test of this kind.*

These charts bear an amazing resemblance to actual futures price charts, with trendlines, reversals, and so forth. And since the patterns were generated by a completely random process, it would have been impossible at any point to make meaningful predictions about what would happen next.

Random walk advocates contend that this same situation prevails in the futures markets themselves. Technicians such as myself naturally disagree, and evidence such as the USDA study mentioned previously seems to support the hypothesis of non-randomness. Still, it is clear that futures price changes are in some sense nearly random— especially over the very short term, which means that the technician's tools must be very carefully chosen and applied if he hopes to profit from the non-randomness.

Suiting Techniques to One's Temperament

There are probably almost as many ways of trading the commodity markets as there are commodity traders. Not every method is suited to the temperament of all traders. An automatic trend method that yields consistent annual profits to a well-disciplined part-time trader may fail in the hands of a more experienced full-time trader who often tries to outsmart his own system, and therefore finds it impossible to stick to the mechanical rules. A system of scale-up and scaledown trading against the immediate trend that works well for a cool, calculating, and unemotional trader with ample reserve funds may prove disastrous for a trader who lacks those psychological qualifications.

It is quite important for a trader to determine the program of action that best suits his temperament and bankroll, and is thus most likely to prove profitable for him in actual practice. The techniques described in this book should be viewed with that principle in mind. One can hardly expect to successfully utilize every known technical tool in his daily trading, and it is questionable whether such a course would insure greater success than could be achieved through a careful selection of a limited number of appropriate techniques. It is hardly necessary to point out that *the tools that seem to serve one best are the tools best used.*

It is almost certain that new techniques will continue to be discovered, and that improved variations of old techniques will be developed. Every chart trader owes it to himself to seek to expand on old techniques and to keep searching for new ones. Although perfection in commodity trading may be unattainable, consistent improvement is certainly a goal within reach.

One of the oldest chart techniques is based on interpreting the patterns or formations that evolve on daily high-low-close charts. This is the subject of the next chapter.

CHAPTER **2**

The Interpretation of
Chart Formations

The Essential Ingredient of all Chart Formations

It was pointed out at the beginning of Chapter 1 that price chart analysis could be summed up in one word—"TREND." The earliest published technical comments on price movements were those of Charles Henry Dow, who created the original Dow Jones stock averages in 1897 and analyzed their price movements in the columns of the *Wall Street Journal.* His observation that a succession of ascending highs and ascending lows was characteristic of a bull trend and that descending tops and descending bottoms were bearish, familiar as it may sound today, was quite an innovation at the time, and later became one of the main ingredients of the "Dow Theory." The fact is that prices rarely move straight up or straight down. They usually waver and react along the way. The result is a series of waves or zigzags within the prevailing trend.

This zigzag pattern is the foundation of all chart formations, and is the key to their forecasting value.

Since there are always small trends moving within larger trends, and large trends moving within still larger ones, it is important to consider each trend in relation to the next larger trend of which it is part. *All chart formations are some variation of either the minor or major zigzag trend pattern,* and should therefore be viewed in that light regardless of what name one might apply to the formation.

Defining the Minor and Major Trends

Trends are often difficult to pin down, and the terms "minor" and "major" may have different meanings to different persons. It is not essential that everyone agree on the same precise definition. However, a technician should have a clear concept of what *he* considers minor and major trends if he intends to take trading action on the basis of the direction of those trends.

Trendlines comprise one of the tools that can be used for identifying trends, and will be discussed at length in the next chapter. The constant-width curved channel, which will also be described in a later chapter, is another means of identifying small and large trends. In this section we are concerned only with the relationship between the zigzag patterns of the market and trends.

To begin, we must select a price or prices to use. Some traders plot only the daily close, and use the swings of closing prices as guides to the direction of the minor trend. However, the swings of the daily high-low ranges, I believe, are perhaps more practical for that purpose. The following "definition" is therefore suggested:

We can start by asserting that the minor trend itself contains a still smaller trend of day-to-day changes. These we will label the "daily" trend. If today's high and low are higher than yesterday's high and low, the daily trend is up; and, if today's range is similarly below yesterday's, the daily trend is down. The "up" days and "down" days, in the course of time, form a zigzag pattern that can be used as a basis for determining the direction of the minor trend, as shown in figs. 3A and 3B.

But what about "inside" and "outside" days? An inside day (when the daily price range is within the high-low range of the previous day) is easy to label. An inside day changes nothing, and can be considered as simply a continuation of the previous day's daily trend. Outside days (when the range extends both above and below

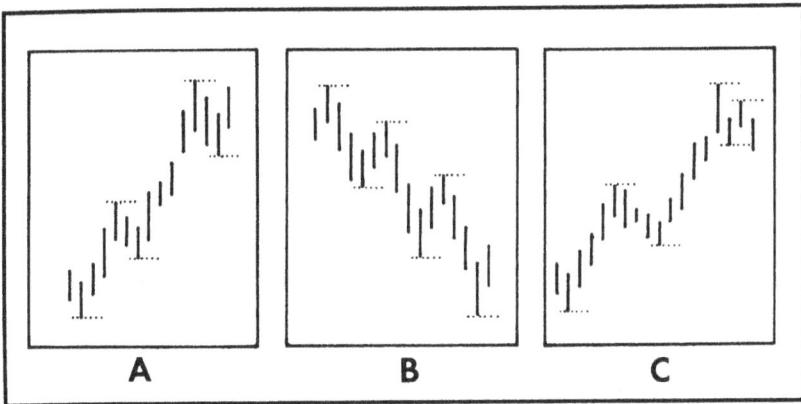

Figure 3A.   **Figure 3B.**   **Figure 3C.**
Minor Uptrend   Minor Downtrend   Minor Trend Variation

Figure 3. Minor Trend Patterns: When the daily zigzag movements of a market show ascending highs and ascending lows the minor trend is upward, as in Figure 3A. Descending highs and descending lows define a minor downtrend, as in Figure 3B. However, personal judgement must sometimes be used to evaluate the zigzag movements. In Figure 3C the final three-day downward zigzag is so out of step with the previous broader price swings that it is best treated as a single downswing within the minor uptrend.

the previous day's range) are not so easily labeled. In most cases, an outside day can be treated in the same way as an inside day—as a continuation of the previous day's daily trend. However, in the case of an outside day, the closing price becomes important. If the closing price of an outside day decisively reverses the trend of the previous day (based on that previous day's close), then the outside day should be labeled as a reversal of the previous day's trend. Sometimes the outside day even reacts far enough to reverse the minor trend itself.

Once the treatment of inside and outside days has been settled, the definition of the minor trend is almost resolved. There is still one other variation that must be considered, and that is the treatment of a succession of alternate up and down days (or similar irregular pattern) that is out of rhythm with the previous zigzag cycles of the minor move. For example, as shown in fig. 3C, let us suppose that there have been two up-legs so far, the first containing four up days followed by four down days, and the second containing another five up days; but then we get a down day and an up day followed by another down day that goes below the low of the previous day. By strict interpretation, the minor trend has now turned down, but the one-day reversal of the daily trend is so out of step with the previous pattern that the last three days are best treated as a series of down days within the uptrend—a reaction within the minor advance.

This aspect of interpretation resists precise definition, and is best left to the chartist's own individual judgment. The rule of "up" and "down" days, used as a basic guide to the direction of the minor trend, should also be applied with discretion.

Once the minor trend has been identified, it is relatively simple to identify the next larger trend, which we will call the "major" trend. Just as the minor trend was composed of the zigzag swings of daily up and down days, the major trend is composed of the zigzag swings of the minor uptrends and minor downtrends. A succession of minor up and down trends making higher tops and higher bottoms produces a major uptrend, while descending minor tops and bottoms identify a major downtrend.

In both major and minor trends, for an uptrend to reverse to a downtrend, the signal is most convincing when a high falls short of the previous high before the price drops below the previous low, since this results in a lower top and a lower bottom. Nevertheless, a downside penetration that comes from a higher top should also be considered valid as an indication of a downturn.

Similarly, in a downtrend, the failure to make a new low followed by a rally above the previous high would be a more convincing reversal than a new high coming after a new low. Both signals, however, would be valid indications of a turn in trend. It should be kept in mind also that any trend reversal that runs counter to the direction of the next larger trend may prove to be of short duration.

Chart Formations as a Function of the Trend

As prices zigzag their way up, down, or sideways, their day-to-day movements trace out many formations or patterns on the charts. The observation and study of those patterns over the years has shown that certain of them tend to give reliable clues to the future direction of prices. Among the formations that are well-known to most chartists, I believe the most dependable are the head-and-shoulders tops and bottoms, sideways consolidations, rounding or "saucer" tops and bottoms, double tops and bottoms, expanding tops and bottoms, and flag patterns. Each one of these formations could be interpreted strictly on the basis of zigzag price swings, without labeling the formation with a name, and essentially the same trend forecast would be made. The recognition of a familiar formation, however, gives the chartist further assurance of a correct trend analysis.

Nevertheless, an undue concentration on chart formations without paying proper attention to their internal trend characteristics can lead one to see formations where they do not actually exist. *For a chart formation to have valid forecasting value, it must be composed of minor and daily trends that could themselves signal the next direction of the trend.*

The importance of the zigzag trend pattern within a chart formation is apparent in the chart of February 1976 Live Cattle as shown in fig. 4. Note that after making a higher bottom at A, the market advanced to a new high at B. At this stage, the action is still bullish. The subsequent downward reaction to C again held bullishly above the previous low, but the failure of the high at D to exceed the previous high was reason for the bulls to be concerned. When the subsequent decline ultimately penetrated the low that was made at C, the trend of the past three months was reversed from up to down.

It is not really necessary to give this top formation a name, since the zigzag pattern speaks for itself, but several possibilities are apparent. It could be labeled a head-and-shoulders top, as shown in fig. 5. In that formation, the downside penetration of the neckline would have given a slightly earlier bear signal than the penetration of the low at C.

The formation could also be labeled a triangle, as depicted in fig. 6. The higher low at C and the lower high at D qualify this formation to be called a triangle. Again, the downside penetration of the lower trendline would have given an early and valid bear signal.

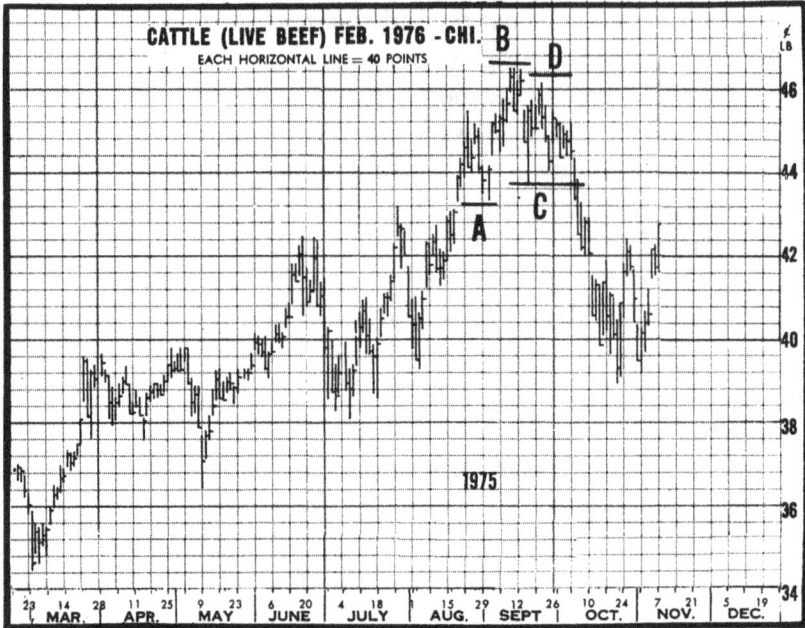

Figure 4. Minor Top Formation: When the pattern of ascending highs and lows changed to a pattern of descending highs and lows, a top formation took shape. At points A, B, and C the zigzag pattern was still bullish. When the rally to D failed to carry above the previous high at B and prices broke through the low at C, the trend turned down. Whatever name the chartist might assign to this formation, the trend change is reflected in the change in direction of the zigzag swings.

Finally, in fig. 7 one can visualize a so-called "diamond" formation, since each one of the four lines of this formation makes contact at two clearly defined price reversal points. Here again, the downside penetration of a trendline gave a bear signal.

While the identification of these formations may have been helpful in anticipating this top, their development was due entirely to the change in direction of the minor swings as the patterns were being completed.

The Classic Chart Formations

Most chartists need no introduction to the classic chart formations, which have been well publicized over the years. The following review of a few of the better known formations is included here merely as a "refresher course," and to tie them in with other techniques recommended in this text.

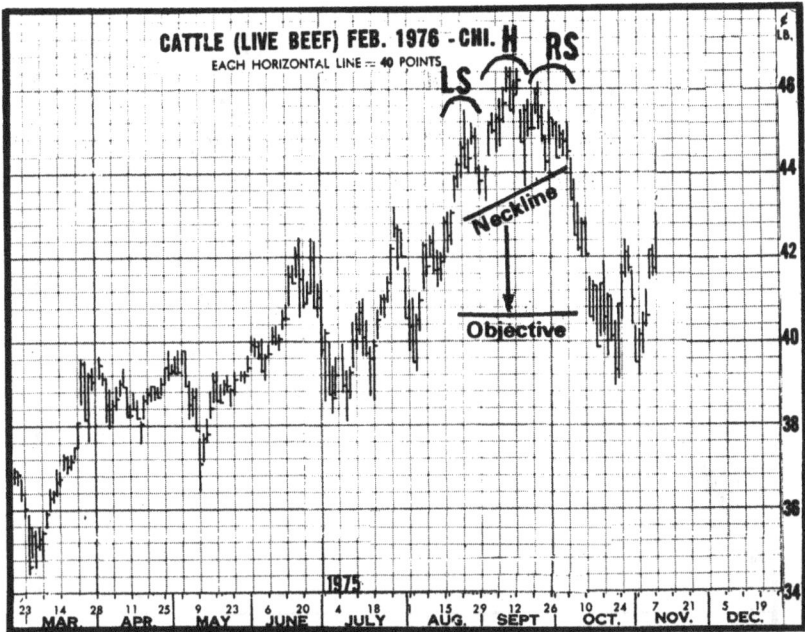

Figure 5. Head-and-shoulders Top: This is the same top formation shown in Figure 4. There is a left shoulder, a right shoulder, and a head between them. The dips on each side of the head are the "armpits." The trendline across the armpits is called the "neckline." The downside objective measurement is the vertical distance from the head to the neckline projected downward from the neckline. A Head-and-Shoulders formation is always composed of zigzag swings that reveal the change in direction of the trend.

Among the most reliable chart patterns in the group is the *head-and-shoulders* formation. In a head-and-shoulders top (fig. 5), the left shoulder and the head are a continuation of the bullish pattern of ascending highs. Unless the descent from the "head" cuts through an uptrend line or the previous low there is no clear advance warning of a top. The right shoulder takes shape when the next upswing falls short of the last high (the head) and then starts down. However, the formation cannot be considered a head-and-shoulders top until it is completed by a downside penetration of the "neckline" or the low at the right "armpit." The two "armpits," of course, are the dips on either side of the head, and the "neckline" is a trendline drawn across the lows of the two armpits. Some head-and-shoulders formations contain multiple heads or multiple shoulders that may

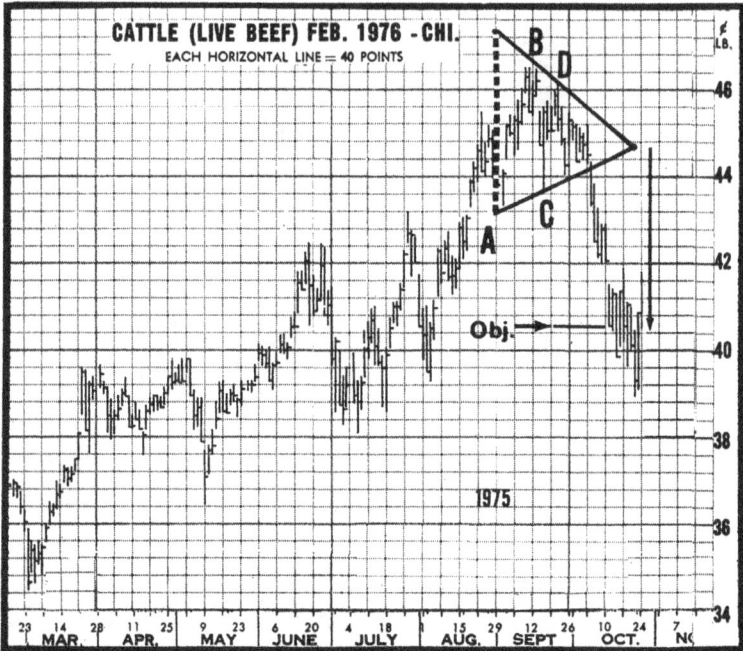

Figure 6. Triangle Formation: The top formation shown in Figures 4 and 5 can also be treated as a Triangle Formation. The higher bottom at C made it possible to draw an uptrend line, while the lower top at D was used for a downtrend line. The two lines converged at the apex of a triangle. The left side of the triangle was formed by drawing a vertical line upward from point A. A downside objective could be projected by taking the vertical height of the triangle at point A and measuring the same distance downward from the apex of the triangle. As with all price formations, the zigzag swings themselves are consonant with the change in trend.

make the formation more difficult to identify, but the tendency is toward symmetry: a formation with two left shoulders, for example, is likely also to develop two right shoulders.

One contingency to guard against is the possibility that a minor head-and-shoulders top may be followed by only a short-lived (minor) decline within a major uptrend, and then evolve into a potentially bullish flag-like formation. A head-and-shoulders top, like all formations, must always be viewed in relation to its position within the minor, major, and long-term trends in progress at the time the pattern develops.

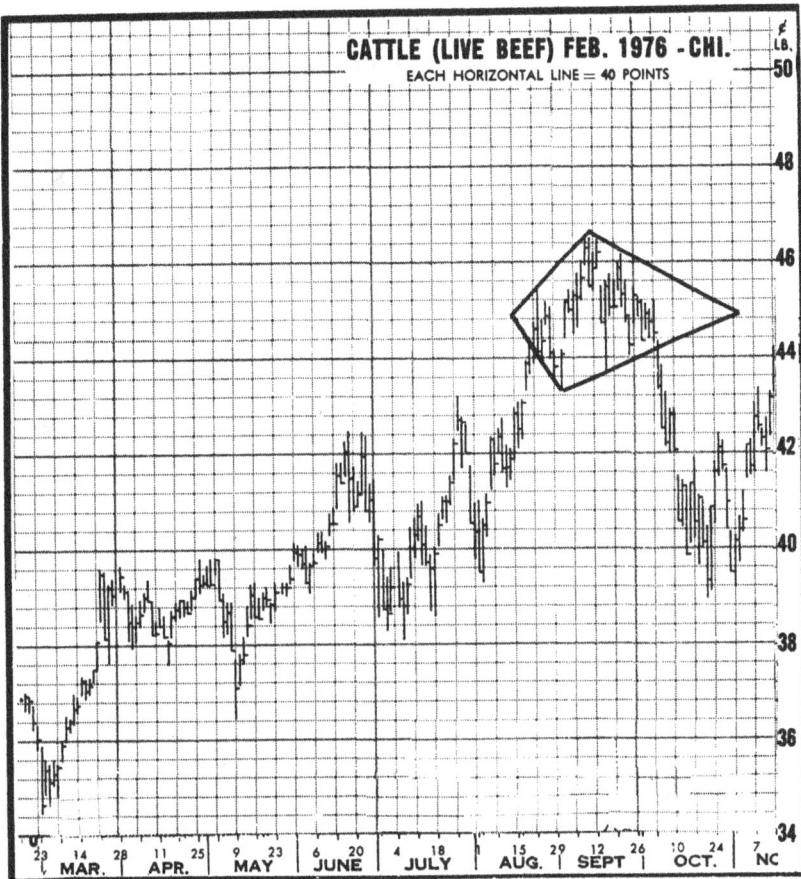

Figure 7. Diamond Formation: The same top formation shown in the three previous charts could also be called a Diamond Formation. Each of the four lines is drawn across two projecting price swings. The downside penetration of the lower uptrend line signaled the downturn.

In a head-and-shoulders bottom the formation is inverted and all the above principles apply in the reverse direction.

The more massive the head-and-shoulders formation, the more power it has to propel the next move. After the signal has been given by the penetration of the neckline, there is sometimes a return move back to the neckline before the main move gets under way in the direction signaled. A completed head-and-shoulders formation may be followed by a very extensive price move, and its short-term potential can be estimated by measuring the vertical distance from the outermost point of the head to the neckline, and projecting that distance vertically from the neckline. An example of this measurement can be seen in the head-and-shoulders bottom in the chart of November 1975 Soybeans in fig. 8. After achieving the measured upside objective and reacting, the market proceeded to new highs. In fig. 9 (July 1972 Cotton), a minor head-and-shoulders top can be seen. The minor top took shape within a long-term advance, and the measured downside objective was not quite reached when the long-term uptrend was resumed.

A *flag* formation is a temporary "corrective" reaction within the trend. To be worthy of its name, a flag must "wave" from a "flagpole." In a bull trend, the flag is a relatively sluggish downward zig-

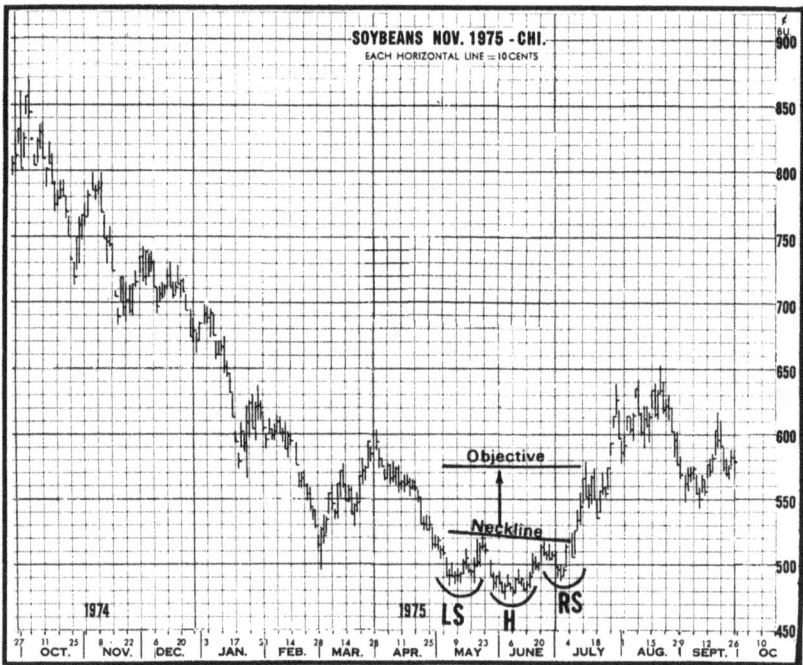

Figure 8. Head-and-shoulders Bottom: Following a prolonged price decline a Head-and-Shoulders bottom signaled the trend change. The formation took more than two months to complete. The head, of course, is at the bottom. The trendline across the two "armpits" enabled one to project an initial upside target, at which level the market reacted before resuming its upward course.

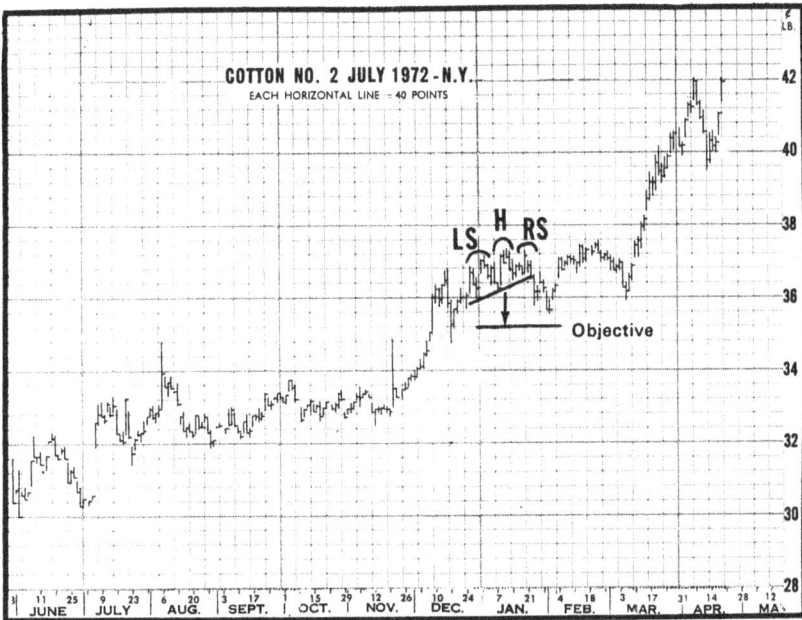

Figure 9. Minor Head-and-shoulders Top: This small top formation was made up of minor zigzag price swings and therefore gave only a minor bear signal within a major uptrend. Chart formations must always be evaluated for their relative importance within the minor, major, and long-term trends that are in progress at the time.

zag pattern following a steep and rapid advance. The flag formation is not complete until the downward zigzag pattern is reversed by an upside penetration of a previous high swing within the formation. Once that occurs, it can be taken as evidence that the downward correction has ended and that the bull trend has been resumed. The upturn out of a downward flag can also be signaled by the upside penetration of a trendline, and this aspect is discussed further in Chapter 3 in the section on "Reaction Trendlines." In a downtrend, potentially bearish flags wave upward, and the same technical principles apply in the reverse direction. An example of a large, downward waving flag in a major bull trend is shown in the chart of November 1978 Plywood in fig. 10.

Double tops and double bottoms are also known as "M" and "W" formations. In a double top, the initial downward reaction from the high of the bull move is followed by a rally that retraces the entire

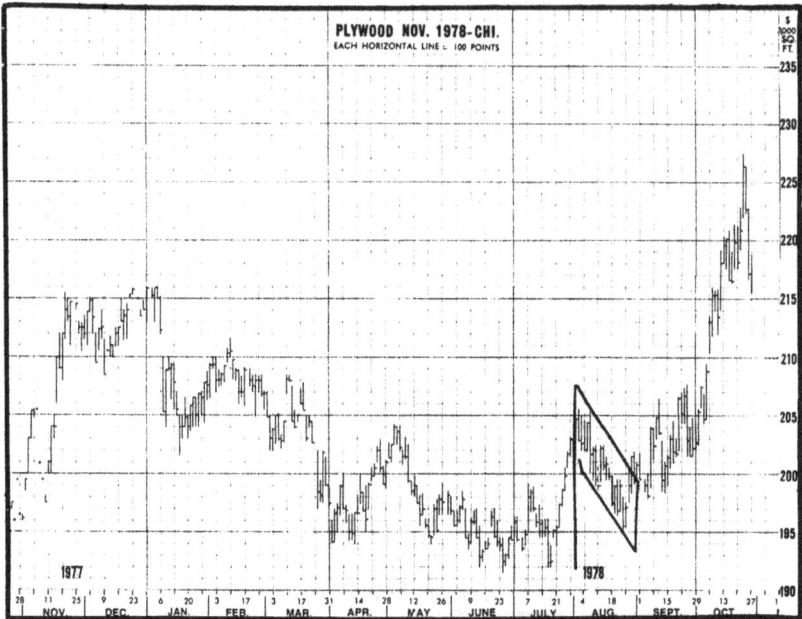

Figure 10. Large Downward Flag Within a Bull Trend: The steep and rapid advance from the July low formed the "flagpole." The slow zigzagging decline in August formed the waving "flag." The formation gave promise of being bullish but was not completed until the price broke out on the upside at the end of August, thus giving a bull signal.

downward reaction. It is not necessary for both highs of the double top to be at precisely the same price level, but they should line up very closely. The second top could even be very slightly above the first. The formation is completed when the decline from the second top falls below the low of the initial downward reaction and closes there, thus giving a bear signal. Until that downside penetration occurs, the formation is not a valid double top.

Of course, as soon as the second top begins to show clear signs of backing away from the level of the first top, it would be suspiciously bearish action. This would give the chart technician good reason to view the chart pattern as a potential double top, and perhaps to take cautious action accordingly. Double bottoms develop in the same manner in the opposite direction.

A typical example of a double top can be seen in the chart of April 1976 Platinum, fig. 11. It is interesting to note that before the sec-

Figure 11. Double Top: When prices began to back away from the second top it was suspiciously bearish action, but the formation was not completed until the bear signal was given by a penetration of the mid-August low. Note that before the second top was made the formation could have been interpreted as a bullish flag. This demonstrates the importance of constantly watching the progress of the large and small zigzag swings for signs of a change in trend.

ond top was made, the formation could have been interpreted as a bullish flag. This illustrates the importance of constantly watching the progress of the large and small zigzag swings for signs of a change in trend. In this connection, note the bearish "drift pattern" at the second top, described later in this chapter and illustrated on this same chart in fig. 16.

Sideways consolidations are sometimes very similar to double tops or double bottoms, but may occur as either reversal or continuation patterns. In Dow Theory terminology, a sideways consolidation is known as a "line." A sideways, trendless price movement is sometimes called a sideways consolidation, but by strict definition it should contain at least two highs and two lows; in other words, it should be a combination of a double top and a double bottom. A penetration and close beyond the outermost high or low of the consolidation formation signals the direction of the next price move. The bottom formation in May 1978 Pork Bellies shown in fig. 12 qualifies as both a sideways consolidation and a double bottom.

Triangles are actually a variation of the sideways consolidation,

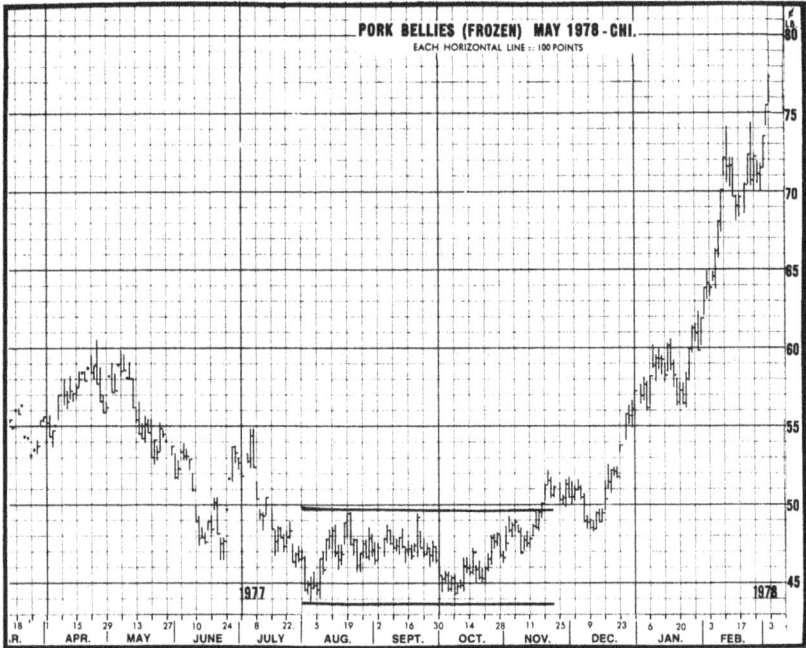

Figure 12. Sideways Consolidation: Note the double tops and double bottoms that are characteristic of a well-defined sideways formation. The bull signal was given in mid-November when the price advanced above the double top and closed there.

since the trend is neither up nor down but sideways. Except for the ascending (flat-top) triangle and the descending (flat-bottom) triangle, every triangle must contain at least one lower top and one higher bottom. Trendlines across the descending tops and the ascending bottoms converge to form the apex of the triangle. The breakout through either the upper or lower trendline of the triangle signals the probable direction of the next price move. However, as with all formations, the minor swings of prices are all-important, and must be watched closely before and after breakout for confirmation of the trend. Triangles usually occur as continuation patterns— pauses within the trend—but can also develop into important tops or bottoms. (For a measuring technique, see "The Triangle Measurement" in Chapter 5).

While most top or bottom formations contain rather volatile

price swings within their structure, the *rounding or "saucer" top or bottom* is notable for its slow, dull action, with prices showing little vigor in either direction. There is usually a series of shallow zigzag swings that gradually bend around from the old direction to the new, finally giving the reversal signal when one of the counter-trend reaction swings goes beyond the extreme of the previous reaction. Whether or not one recognizes the formation as a "saucer," the change in the direction of the minor swings will signal the reversal of trend.

Expanding tops and bottoms do not occur frequently, which is per- haps fortunate, since they are actually a whipsaw pattern in which two false signals are followed by a third valid signal. The formation

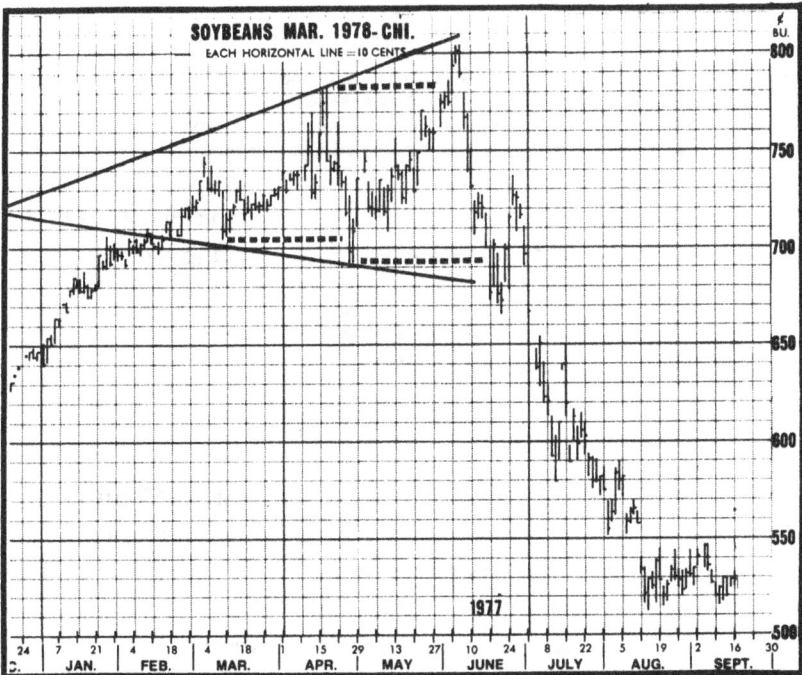

Figure 13. Expanding Top: A false downside penetration in late April was fol- lowed by a false upside penetration to a new high and then by a valid downside penetration in June. This type of formation does not occur frequently, which is perhaps fortunate. There is no foolproof remedy for avoiding the two whipsaws, because the formation cannot be readily recognized until after the third (and only valid) reversal signal.

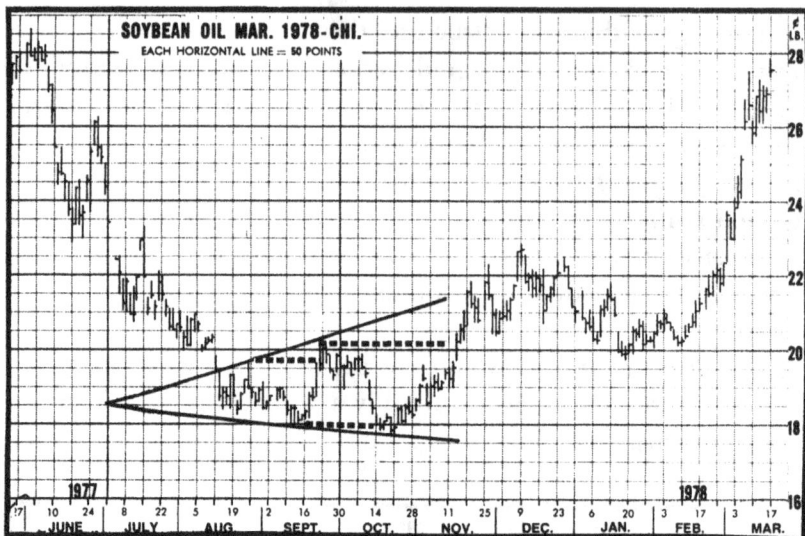

Figure 14. Expanding Bottom: A premature breakout in September was followed by a bearish new low in October; however, both of these proved to be false signals. The third and valid signal was given when the November advance penetrated the September high, thus completing an Expanding Bottom formation.

is the mirror image of a triangle, with its apex at the left instead of at the right. There is no foolproof remedy for avoiding the two whipsaws, because the formation cannot be readily recognized until after the third reversal signal. An example of an expanding top is shown in fig. 13, and an expanding bottom in fig. 14.

The Magic Number "Three"

The three reversal signals of the expanding top and bottom formation bring to mind a remarkable characteristic of price movements in commodity futures markets. For some reason the number "three" seems to play an important role in commodity price-chart analysis. For example, many major price moves progress in three main stages with two intervening corrective swings (the so-called "Elliott waves" described later in this chapter); when a trendline has to be revised twice and redrawn a third time because of two previous false penetrations, the penetration of the third trendline usually proves to be valid (the classic "fan" formation); dynamic moves up or down often contain three main gap varieties: a breakaway gap, midway or runaway gaps, and an exhaustion gap (all of which are discussed later in this chapter); in the day-to-day progress of most trends, the brief reactions along the way often form a tight, overlapping three-day pattern—a miniature "flag"—that is followed by a resumption of the trend. For whatever reason, this triplet tendency shows up repeatedly in the commodity markets.

The "Drift" Pattern

Commodity chart technicians who watch the day-to-day action of the markets closely can get advance warning of an impending change in trend from an awareness of the "drift" pattern, which is in my opinion one of the most important chart formations. A drift pattern may be defined as a series of upward or downward days during which time the market just drifts along, with each day's range substantially overlapping the range of the previous day. The three-day reaction pattern described in the previous section is actually one example of a drift pattern.

In an uptrend, one can expect the upward price action to be somewhat more vigorous than the temporary downward reactions, while in a downtrend downward price movements are likely to be the more dynamic. As a result, prices usually tend to run swiftly in the direction of the immediate trend, and to "drift" slowly in the opposite direction. The resulting chart picture sometimes resembles a series of miniature flag formations, each on its own small flagpole. The value of the drift pattern lies in the fact that it helps the chartist determine on a *day-to-day* basis whether the immediate character of the market is potentially bullish or potentially bearish. If during an upward move the pattern should change from an upward "run" to an upward "drift," that would be a danger signal, and *any slight downturn from that small upward drift would be suspiciously bearish.* If the downturn should be a sharp drop, it would be further confirmation of bearishness, while a downward drift that follows an upward drift reinstates the bullish potential.

Some examples of small drift patterns that give a key to the imme-

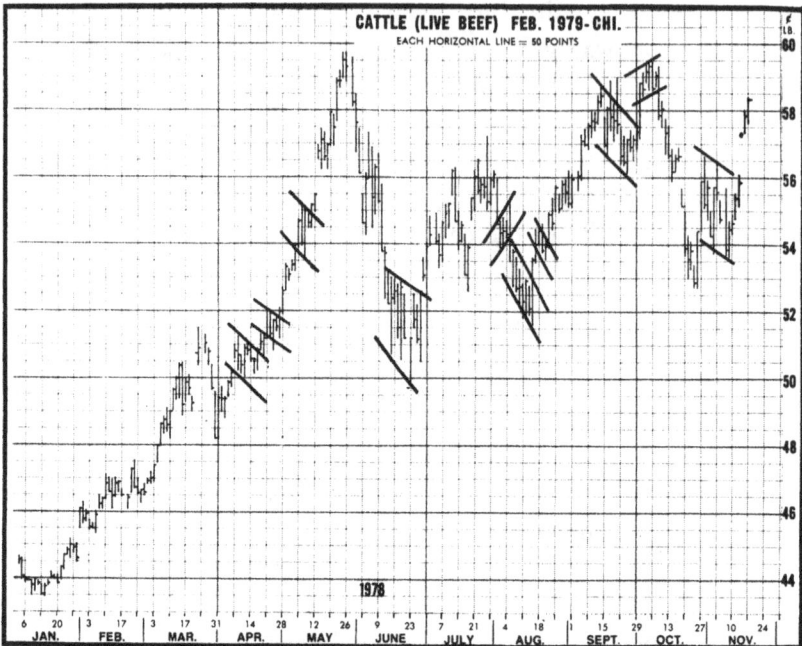

Figure 15. Drift Patterns: Prices usually move more vigorously in the direction of the immediate trend. Sluggish counter-trend movements often form Drift Patterns consisting of three or more days of overlapping daily ranges. Downward drifts are potentially bullish; upward drifts are potentially bearish.

diate direction of prices by running counter to the immediate trend are shown in the charts of February 1979 Live Beef Cattle (fig. 15) and April 1976 Platinum (fig. 16). In the April Platinum chart note the potentially bearish four-day upward drift at the high in late August. This is the same double top that was shown in fig. 11.

It must be emphasized that a drift pattern in itself does not give a positive signal. It is an important warning, however, that is confirmed when the price breaks out of the drift pattern. It should be noted, too, that what starts out as a drift can sometimes finish as an accelerating trend in the same direction as the drift.

Just as there are small minor drift patterns formed by the day-to-day action of the market, there are also larger drift patterns of major significance containing the smaller ones. Longer-term trends must therefore also be examined for signs of "run" and "drift." In a major

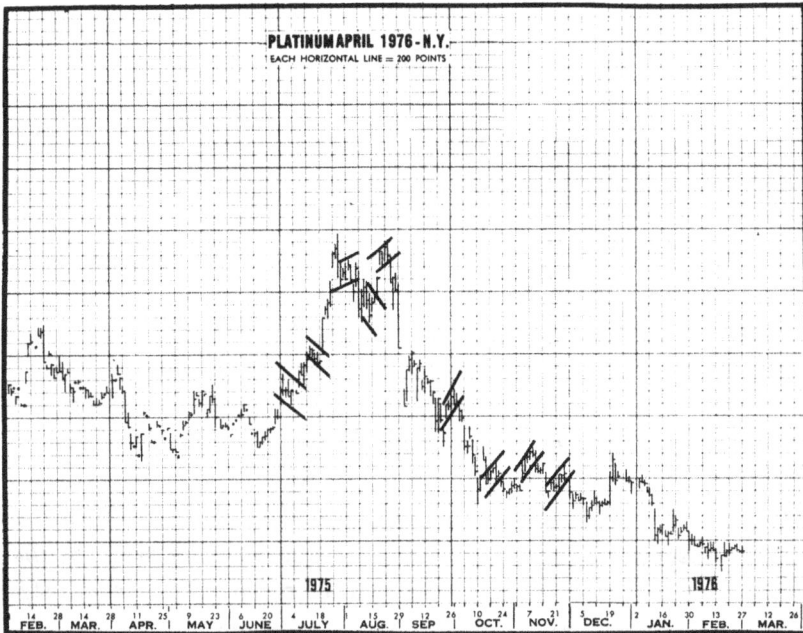

Figure 16. Drift Patterns: Among the Drift Patterns shown on this chart is a potentially bearish upward drift at the high of late August. This is the second top of the Double Top formation previously shown in Figure 11.

bull market, the upward legs tend to be steeper and move faster than the corrective declines. When the advance stops running and starts creeping, it is a warning of a potential downturn ahead. Within that *major* creeping advance, a drift pattern in the *minor* price movement may give a clue to the timing of a downturn. Even though a major upward drift is potentially bearish, it may at first contain bullish minor downdrift patterns within it. If finally the minor pattern begins to drift upward instead of downward, making both the major and minor patterns potentially bearish, it is almost a sure sign of an immediate downturn ahead.

In a major bear market, the same rules apply in the opposite direction. Of course, the markets do not produce a constant flow of drift patterns, and it is useless to try and identify drifts where they do not exist. But they do seem to appear frequently in all markets, and when they do show up they can be of great value to the chartist.

The "Slope" Formation as a Forecasting Tool

The slope formation is a flag that waves in the *same* direction as the prevailing trend instead of waving in the *opposite* direction. It occurs after a steep and rapid move, when market action suddenly slows but continues in the same direction within a broad sloping channel. It is usually a reversal pattern; that is, a top formation in an advancing trend and a bottom formation in a downward move. A typical sloping bottom is shown in the chart of May 1976 Maine Potatoes in fig. 17, and a sloping top appears in the March 1976 Cocoa chart in fig. 18. Note the "flagpole" in both cases.

When the price breaks out of the slope formation and signals a reversal of trend, there is a measurement rule that can be applied to estimate the probable extent of the new move. The rule is that the price is likely to go *beyond the starting point* of the sloping channel and continue in the new direction until it reaches *the next congestion area*. Once that area has been reached, the objective has been satisfied and the predictive powers of the slope are exhausted.

How does one determine when the price has broken out of the formation? A conventional trendline across the slope can be used, but it is sometimes unreliable in this type of formation, as there is a tendency for one or more false penetrations to occur. The zigzag swings within the formation are a more reliable guide, even though the outermost point of a previous swing may give a slightly delayed signal. Another method—one that I prefer—employs a special kind of trendline that is described below as well as in the next chapter under "The Final Predicted Trendline."

Since the slope formation generally forms a well defined channel, a "channel line" should be drawn first (along the left side of the formation), to be used as a guide for drawing a parallel "trendline." The channel line, however, should not be drawn across the outermost swings of the channel, but through the outermost *closing prices*. The trendline should then be drawn exactly parallel to that channel line, across the outermost tip on the other side. The resulting trendline may touch only a *single point*, or it may by chance coincide with

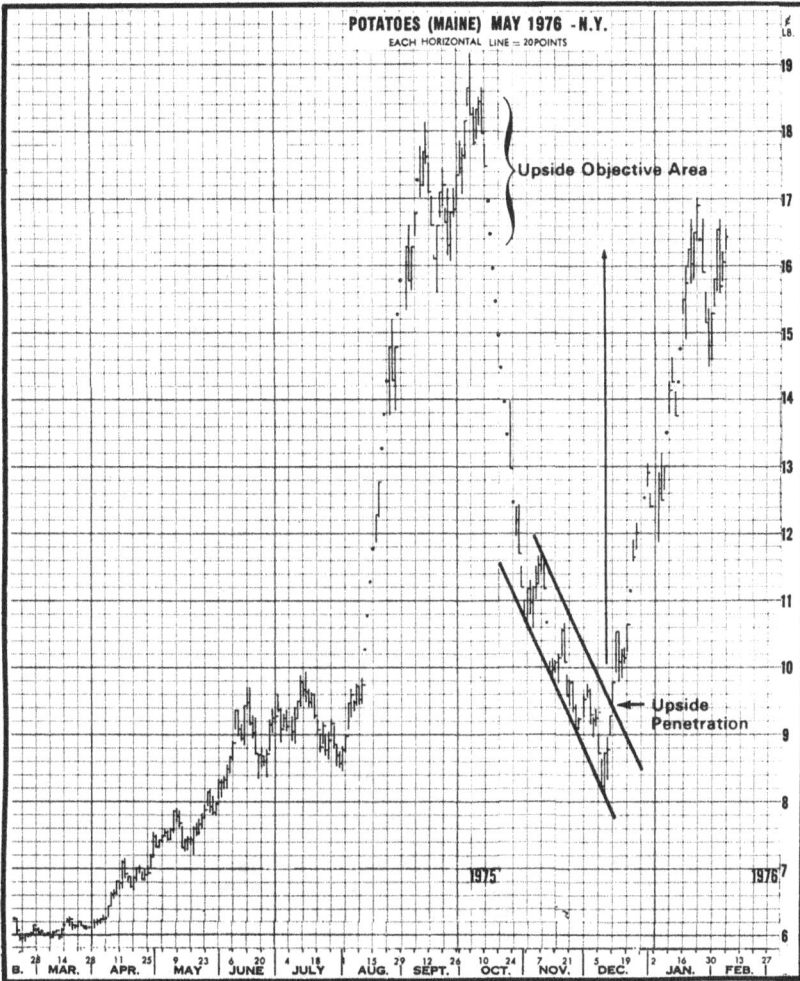

Figure 17. Slope Formation: Note the similarity to a Flag Formation, except that the flag is "waving" in the same direction as the prevailing trend instead of in the opposite direction. A Slope Formation is usually a reversal pattern. A "guideline" was drawn through the low closing prices along the left side of the formation, and a parallel downtrend line was projected across the outermost intraday high on the right, which happened to be the November peak. The upside penetration of that downtrend line gave the bull signal. The upside objective is the first congestion area above the top of the formation.

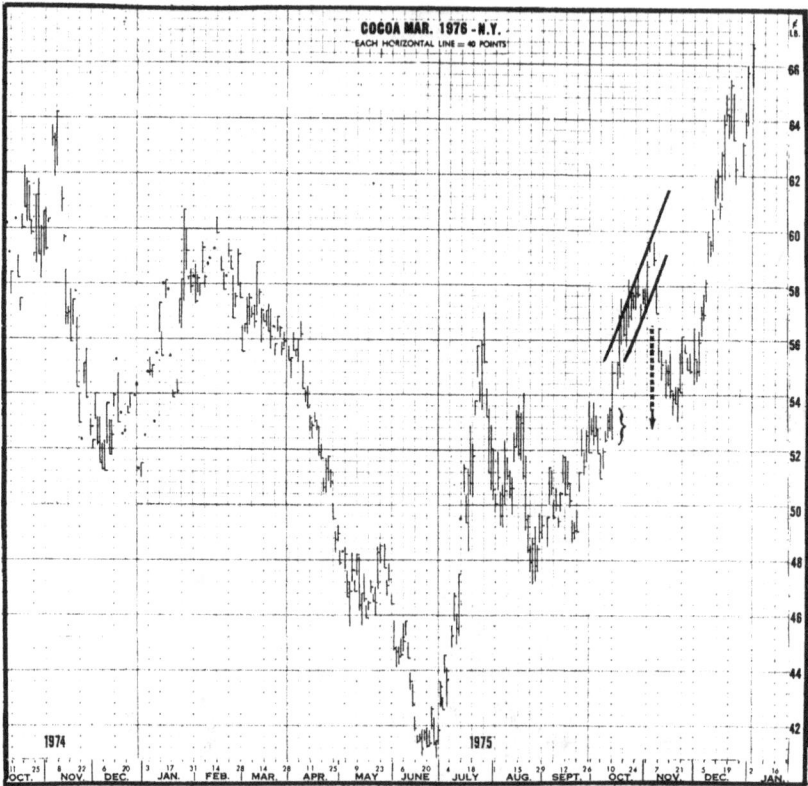

Figure 18. Slope Formation: The steep upswing in mid-October was followed by a small sloping advance. A line drawn through the high closing prices on the left side of the Slope Formation was used as a guide for drawing a parallel uptrend line. The penetration of that uptrend line in early November signaled a decline to an objective within the next support area.

a conventional trendline across two or more points. The penetration of that parallel trendline (when confirmed by a penetration in the close as well) will signal the breakout from the slope.

As already indicated, the slope is usually a potential reversal pattern. However, *the expected reversal should not be taken for granted until it is signaled,* as the formation can occasionally act as a *continuation* pattern.

If the slope is destined to become a continuation pattern, the "creeping" market will begin to "run" in the same direction as the slope, and will no longer remain within the sloping channel. This type of action also has predictive value, since the slope itself then becomes the halfway mark of the price move. The measuring rule is that the subsequent move out of the slope will generally be about equal in magnitude to the steep move that preceded the slope formation.

Gaps that Act as Support and Resistance Areas

A gap can be defined as the blank area left on a bar chart when one day's high-low range is completely above or below the previous day's high-low range. There is a common belief that when a gap occurs it must promptly be "filled" by subsequent price action. In reality this is true only of "common" and "exhaustion" gaps. There are other gaps that tend to resist being filled, and can therefore be treated as support or resistance areas. It should be emphasized that gaps occurring in the less-active, far-off delivery months may not be meaningful, but may simply result from the inactivity of those distant contracts. We are not concerned with such gaps, nor with frequent gaps that occur in any illiquid commodity.

Gaps are generally classified by chartists as "common" gaps, "breakaway" gaps, "midway" or "runaway" gaps, and "exhaustion" gaps. The *common gap* appears most frequently but is of little significance to the chartist. It occurs within congestion areas and during temporary periods of relatively trendless price movement. Common gaps are almost invariably "closed" promptly by subsequent price action, and since common gaps occur so frequently, this probably accounts for the widespread belief that gaps *must* be closed.

The *breakaway gap* occurs at the inception of a trend change. Valid breakaway gaps, unlike common gaps, usually do *not* get filled. If the price subsequently returns toward the breakaway gap, the gap acts as a barrier that repels the correction, and does not permit complete closure to occur. A breakaway gap that *does* get completely covered serves as a warning that a false or premature trend signal may have been given.

Midway or runaway gaps, which generally appear about halfway through a move, also tend to check counter-trend corrections. Some are filled, some are not. It is not easy to distinguish a midway gap from an exhaustion gap at the time it occurs. However, if a tentative price objective was previously determined, and one or more gaps occur about halfway to that objective, those gaps would probably be midway gaps that would reinforce the chartist's measurement of the price objective. Midway gaps that are not promptly filled will usually act as support or resistance after the trend reverses and the market is retracing its previous move.

The *exhaustion gap,* as its name implies, is the result of a final price spurt, and is therefore destined to soon be filled and passed, or perhaps gapped over by a new breakaway gap in the reverse direction.

As a general rule an upside gap that is able to stop a subsequent downward reaction and is not completely filled by the reaction points to further strength ahead. A downside gap that is able to stop a subsequent rally and is not completely filled by the rally points to further weakness ahead. A gap that is completely filled can usually be viewed as a barrier that has been demolished, leaving the market vulnerable to further reversal action.

Characteristics of Opening Gaps

Here is an observation that could prove helpful in timing a trade during the day's session, and in protecting against adverse action that day.

When a market closes *at or near the highs of the day,* and on the following morning gaps up in the opening, the subsequent action *on that day* often follows a certain pattern. As bullish as the initial action may be, the opening strength is usually overdone at the time. Shortly after the opening, the price will usually settle back about *halfway* into the opening gap (providing a buying opportunity) before moving up to new highs for the day. Only in rare instances, such as in a limit-up move on the opening, is the opening gap likely to be left largely intact and uncovered for the day.

While an upside gap on the opening is usually bullish, there can be exceptions. If the opening strength was false, and the market is not destined to close strong that day, the opening gap will be closed completely. Therefore, the reaction back into the gap area after the opening must be watched closely. If the market falls back to the previous close, it would be a warning of false initial strength and of a possible downside reversal at the close. In the case of a downside opening gap following a close at or near the previous day's low, all the above principles apply in the reverse direction.

Some Thoughts on the Elliott Wave Theory

The Elliott wave theory has received increasing attention from chart technicians in recent years. Ralph Nelson Elliott (1871–1947) was an astute observer of stock market price movements. His only known published work, however, was a 64-page book reproduced from his typewritten pages. The book was entitled *Nature's Law— The Secret of the Universe,* and was probably written in 1942 or 1943. The title page shows no publisher's name, and the book appears to have been distributed by Elliott himself from his office at 63 Wall Street in New York City.

The book is a mixture of practical trend analysis and mystical symbolism. Elliott clearly states his belief that there is a rhythm in nature that spills over into all aspects of life on earth, including price movements of stocks and commodities. Once a rhythm has been detected, he indicates, its repetition enables one to predict the future from the past. In one of his introductory statements on rhythm in nature, he says, "Even though we may not understand the cause underlying a particular phenomenon, we can, by observation, predict that phenomenon's recurrence."[1]

In his book Elliott also stresses the importance of the number series known as the "Fibonacci Summation Series." Fibonacci (also known as Leonardo de Pisa) was an Italian mathematician who lived in the 13th Century. Fibonacci's summation series begins with the numbers 1, 1, 2, 3, 5, 8, 13, 21, 34, 55, 89, 144 . . . and goes on to infinity. Except for the first '1,' each number in the series is the sum of the two previous numbers. Elliott was convinced that the num-

[1] Ralph Nelson Elliott, "Nature's Law—The Secret of the Universe," New York, circa 1942, p. 4.

bers in the Fibonacci series were related to all occurrences in nature. Under the heading "Distinctive Features of Human Activities," he lists as No. 1: "All human activities have three distinctive features,—Pattern, Time, and Ratio, all of which observe the Fibonacci Summation Series."[2]

Elliott's explanation of his wave theory in the stock market is confined largely to a 13-page section of the 64-page book, and is based not only on his observations of price movements in the stock market but also on his belief in the importance of rhythms and the Fibonacci numbers.

He describes the ideal or "perfect" market as a major bull market of five waves followed by a major bear market of three waves. Elliott's "wave" is a single upswing or a single downswing of the market. A five-wave bull market, therefore, consists of three up-legs separated by two reaction down-legs. A three-wave bear market consists of a downswing, a rally, and a final downswing. Within the major trends are intermediate trends, which also contain five waves when moving in the same direction as the major trend and three waves when moving counter to the major trend. The intermediate trends, in turn, contain minor trends made up of five waves when moving in the direction of the intermediate trend and three waves when moving counter to the intermediate trend.

The sums of the waves in each uptrend, downtrend, and complete cycle all correspond to Fibonacci numbers, as follows:

	Bull Market	*Bear Market*	*Total Cycle*
Number of major waves	5	3	8
Number of intermediate waves	21	13	34
Number of minor waves	89	55	144

Elliott's diagrams of these perfect wave cycles are reproduced in fig. 19. The waves in the five-wave movements are numbered consecutively 1, 2, 3, 4, and 5, while the three-wave movements are lettered A, B, and C, in accordance with Elliott's practice.

Elliott does not pretend that markets must adhere to these ideal and perfect wave patterns, but he implies that these patterns are the basis for certain variations that occur. The variations, however, are

[2] *Ibid.,* p. 13.

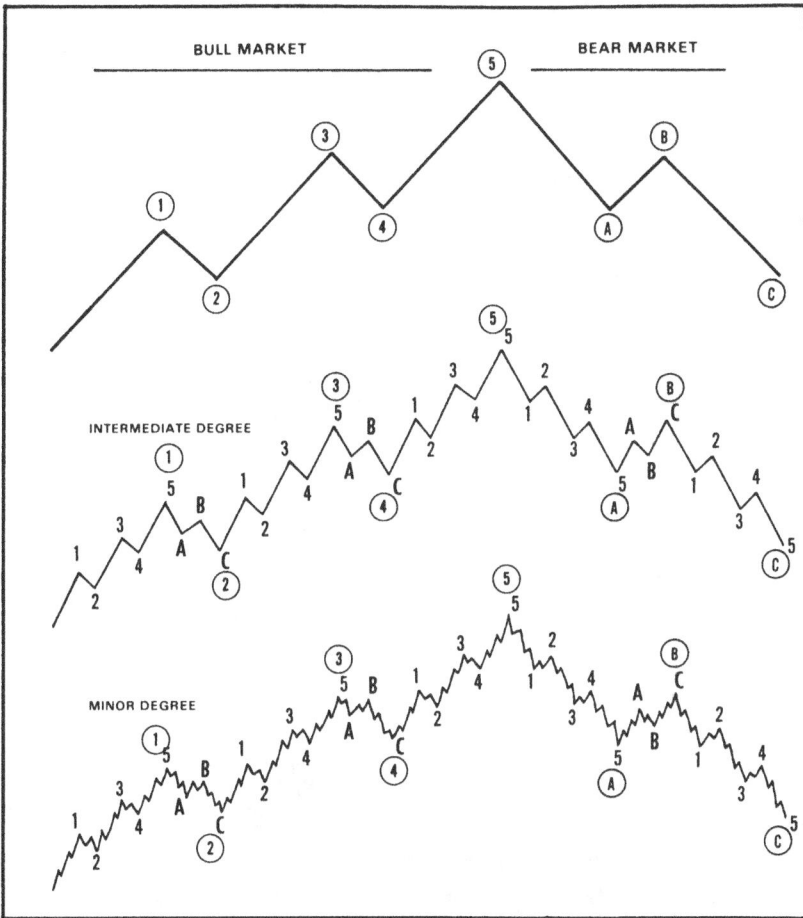

Figure 19. Elliott's Diagram of His Stock Market Wave Cycle: The theoretical make-up of the major, intermediate, and minor trends is shown. Each cycle contains five waves (numbered 1, 2, 3, 4, 5) in the direction of the next larger trend and three waves (lettered A, B, C) in the opposite direction.

quite numerous and complex, and only a few will be described here. Some might be more accurately called exceptions to the rule rather than variations.

The corrective price movements—the three-wave series—are most susceptible to variation, and Elliott warns that corrections in both bull and bear swings are more difficult to learn.

Elliott divides the corrective patterns into three main categories

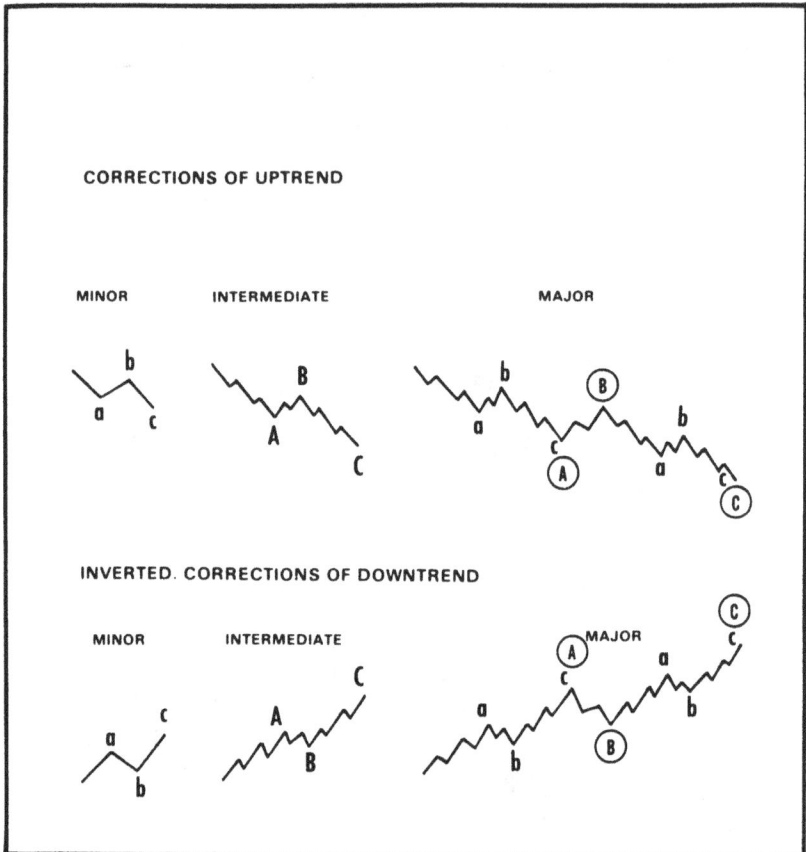

Figure 20. Elliott's Diagram of "Zigzag" Corrections: The three-wave (A, B, C) correction may sometimes take the "zigzag" forms shown here.

which he labels "Zigzag," "Flat" and "Triangle," diagrams of which are shown on this page and the next.

The "Zigzag" correction in a minor trend is a simple three-wave pattern. In an intermediate trend it is a three-wave pattern made up of minor waves in patterns of five, three, and five, consecutively. In a major trend, the "Zigzag" correction contains three major waves, the first and third of which contain intermediate waves in five–three–five order, and the second of which contains an intermediate three-wave reaction. (At this point, it might be noted, the Fib-

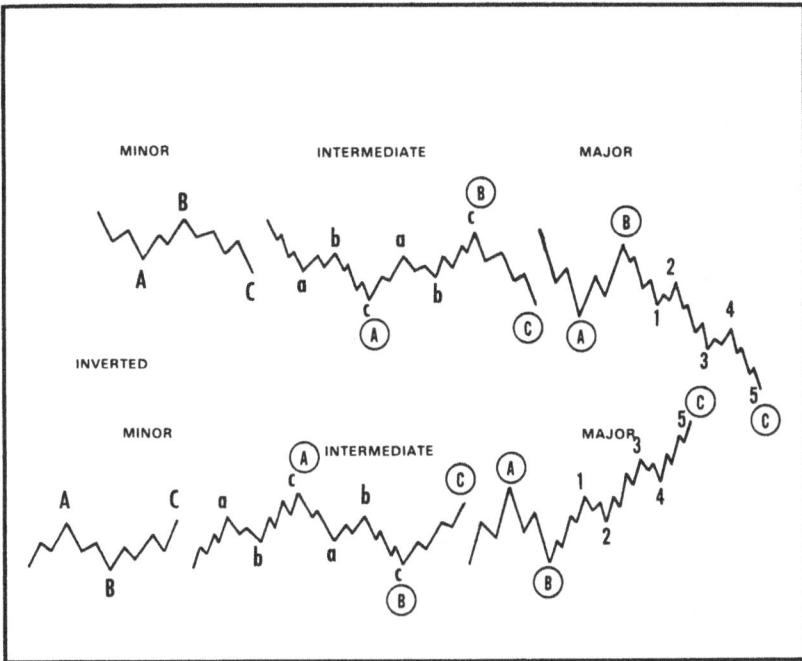

Figure 21. Elliott's Diagram of "Flat" Corrections: This is another variation of the three-wave correction in which additional waves occur within the main waves.

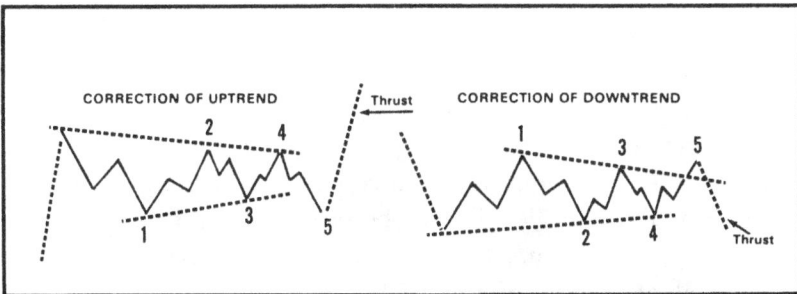

Figure 22. Elliott's Diagram of "Triangle" Corrections: Some corrections take the form of a triangle containing five waves instead of three. The fifth and last wave in the triangle sometimes gives a false signal by breaking out of the triangle prematurely in the wrong direction, followed by a "thrust" in the main direction of the trend. According to Elliott, triangles usually occur as the fourth wave in a five-wave trend and are therefore almost always continuation patterns rather than reversal patterns.

onacci numbers no longer prevail: The sum of waves in a major "Zigzag" correction total 29, about halfway between the Fibonacci numbers 21 and 34.)

The "Flat" corrections are essentially three–three–five wave patterns that move almost sideways and slightly counter to the main trend. A minor "Flat" correction in an intermediate bull market is made up of three waves zigzagging downward, three waves upward, and then five waves downward. In a bear trend the same pattern is followed in the reverse direction: three waves up, three waves down, and five waves up. The intermediate "Flat" correction is a three–three–five wave pattern, with each successive wave containing minor wave patterns of five–three–five, three–three–five, and five waves, consecutively. (The last minor wave pattern is identical to the last intermediate wave pattern.) The major "Flat" three-wave correction contains three intermediate waves in the first major wave, three in the second, and five in the third. The third wave of five intermediate waves also contains minor wave patterns in the sequence of five–three–five–three–five.

The above stereotype format of "Flat" corrections is, of course, an idealized formation that is hardly likely to occur often in real-life markets, and there are some variations that partially cover this contingency. A minor sidewise correction could be composed of more complex forms, such as seven waves (a "double-three") or 11 waves (a "triple-three"). These complex forms are occasionally mixed with both upward and downward zigzags.

"Triangle" corrections are composed of five legs, each of which may or may not be composed of three waves, depending on the relative size of the triangle. Elliott observes that the fifth leg of the triangle may extend outside the trend line of the triangle (giving a false signal of reversal of trend), but will then be followed by a "thrust" in the main direction of the trend. His interpretation of triangles implies that triangles are almost always likely to be continuation patterns rather than reversal patterns, with a false reversal signal sometimes being given. Another interesting observation he made—which could prove to be helpful at times—is that, although triangles occur infrequently, "their position has always been wave 4"[3] (the second reaction) in a five-wave trend.

Elliott describes a number of additional variations of wave forms that contain "extensions," "extensions of extensions," and "enlargements of corrections." Major market tops may occur as "orthodox" tops (the top of the fifth wave); or, as "irregular" tops (a seventh wave at a new high, which in reality is the second "B" wave of the new three-wave bear trend).

Elliott's analysis of stock market price movements in terms of "waves" appears to include just about every possible sequence of price changes that might occur. While some of his wave forms tend to be followed by a predictable price movement, most of the time it would probably be difficult to predict the subsequent action because of the numerous alternative possibilities.

According to Elliott, there is a "key" that should prove helpful in predicting which variation is likely to occur. That key is nature's tendency toward "rhythm" or "alternation." In the stock market, he points out, major "orthodox tops" have always alternated with "irregular tops." If the last major top was "orthodox," the next major top will be "irregular," and the major top following that one will be "orthodox," etc. He explains further that in a five-wave pattern, corrective waves 2 and 4 will alternate in complexity. If wave 2 is simple, wave 4 will be complex; if wave 2 is complex, wave 4 will be simple. By this rule, bull moves and bear moves will not repeat themselves in the same manner twice in succession, but will tend to alternate between one form and another.

The complexities of the Elliott wave theory make positive interpretation difficult and subjective. The waves are not always easy to identify, and it is possible that some charts, when analyzed by different students of the Elliott wave theory, could be given as many different interpretations as there are observers.

Although Elliott makes some brief mention of commodities in his book, his research on "waves" appears to have been confined entirely

---

[3] *Ibid.*, p. 19.

to price movements in the stock market. His typical pattern of a five-wave trend followed by a three-wave reaction can be found in commodity markets, but an examination of commodity price charts covering a cross-section of futures markets at any one time will reveal at least as many exceptions to the rule as similarities.

Perhaps the best way for the commodity chartist to make use of the Elliott wave theory is simply to include it as one of the tools in his kit of chart techniques, applying it in a general way along with his other methods, but always bearing in mind the Rule of Multiple Techniques that requires a chart conclusion to be supported by more than one technique.

For more on Elliott wave theory, see *Concepts on Profits in Commodity Futures Trading,* by Houston A. Cox, Jr., published by Reynolds Securities, Inc., 120 Broadway, New York, N.Y. 10005.

Now let's go back and take closer looks at trendlines, and some conventional and unconventional ways to work with them.

CHAPTER **3**

Trendline Techniques

The Conventional Trendline—A Valuable Tool

Most chart technicians find trendlines to be one of the most valuable tools available. Rarely is there an important change in price trend that is not accompanied by a penetration of a trendline on the daily bar chart. However, trendlines are often penetrated prematurely, and considerable judgment must be exercised in deciding where to place a trendline and in determining when a valid penetration has occurred. If consideration is given to other technical indicators that are applicable to the immediate situation—as required by the Rule of Multiple Techniques—the validity of a trendline penetration can be better evaluated. To some extent, the proper placing of a trendline is an "art," depending on one's own special techniques or on one's recollection of past experiences in similar market situations.

In an uptrend, the conventional trendline is usually drawn across the protruding lows of successive dips, and in a downtrend across the extreme highs of the rallies. It is generally advisable to delay placing a trendline across a point until that point has been firmly established as an intermediate low or high by subsequent market action. In an uptrend this means waiting for the price to approach or penetrate the previous high, while in a downtrend the rally high should not be considered a final trendline point until the price approaches or penetrates the previous low. Another precaution is to consider a penetration of a trendline during the trading session as tentative *until confirmed by the close*. However, no matter what procedure is followed, the possibility of a false penetration cannot be ruled out, and trendlines must sometimes be revised.

To illustrate both the effectiveness and the limitations of conventional trendlines, I have drawn what I consider to be the appropriate trendlines on the daily charts of a number of commodities (shown in figs. 23–28), all covering approximately the same calendar period. The dotted lines indicate where trendlines might have been drawn prematurely; the solid lines are the valid trendlines for the "minor" trends; and the double lines, where drawn, are trendlines for "major" trends.

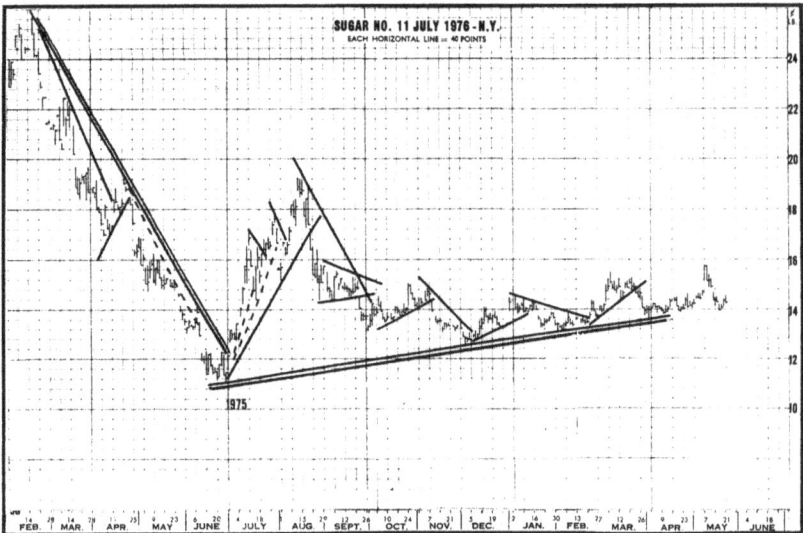

Figure 23. Conventional Trendlines: Personal judgement must be used when drawing trendlines. It is usually best to wait until a price extreme has been clearly established before drawing a trendline across that point. The dotted lines here show trendlines that proved to be false or premature; the single lines represent minor trendlines; the double lines define the major trend.

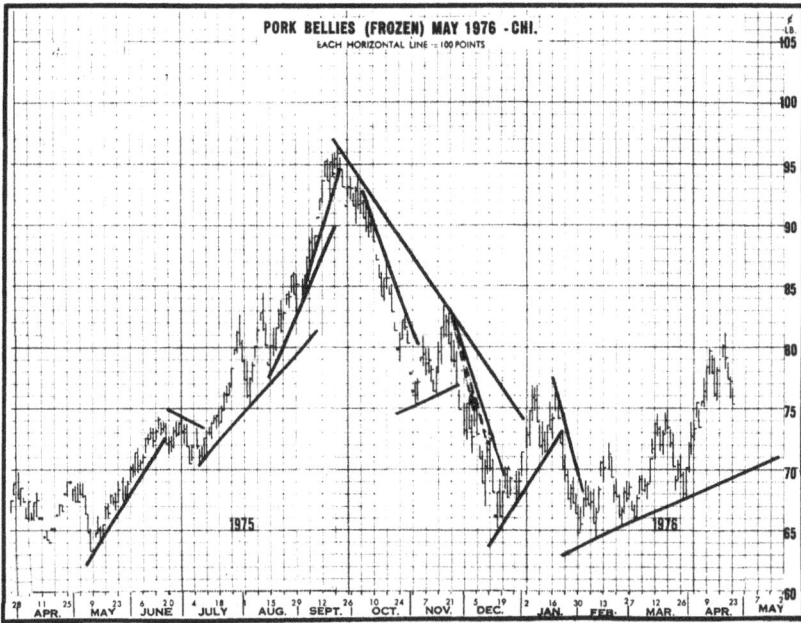

Figure 24. Conventional Trendlines: With few exceptions this volatile market responded well to the application of minor trendlines. During the July-September advance the trendline could have been revised twice to a steeper angle. It eventually caught the downturn very close to the peak.

It can be seen on these charts that there were several occasions when premature trendlines might have been drawn twice in succession, followed by a valid trendline on the third attempt. These are the classic "fan" formations, in which two false penetrations are followed by a third penetration that is valid and meaningful.

It will be seen that all trendlines were drawn only after a counter-trend reaction occurred and appeared to be completed. One cannot precisely define a reaction and its completion, and therefore personal judgment must come into play. If the chartist has reason to believe that the move is in its very early stages, he might delay drawing a trendline until the reaction has been clearly established and left well behind, and he might ignore relatively small price movements. If the trend is thought to be in its final stage, the chartist might choose to draw a tight trendline across any small reaction as soon as it appears

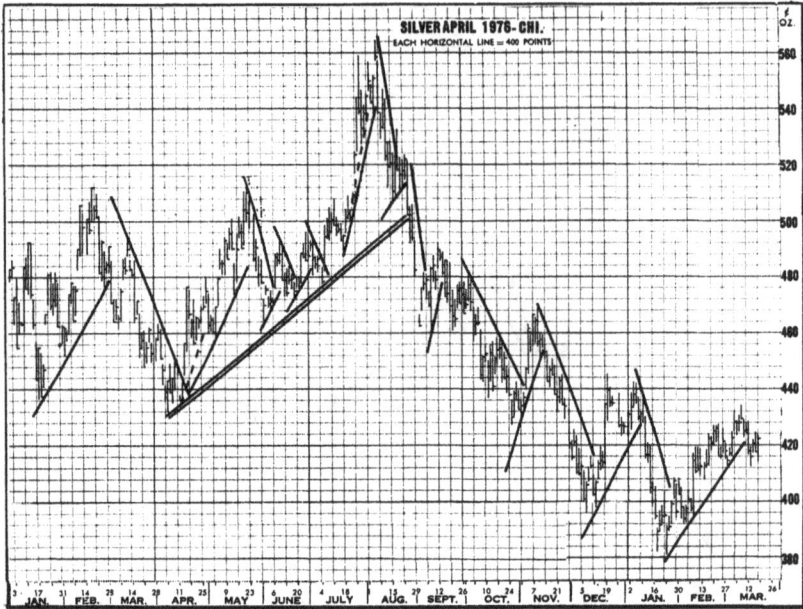

Figure 25. Conventional Trendlines: The erratic price movements in silver made it difficult to correctly position the minor trendlines. Nevertheless, the use of trendlines effectively limited the risk during whipsaws and served well as a means of catching short-term profits.

to have halted. The decision as to whether the trend is in its early or final stages would depend on one's total view of that market, based on chart analysis and perhaps influenced by fundamentals.

The use of trendlines on the long-term weekly continuation charts is discussed in Chapter 9.

Trendlines can often be effectively applied in unconventional ways. The more one experiments with them on the charts, the more useful possibilities come to light. Some unconventional trendline techniques that may be found helpful will be described in this chapter and in Chapter 6 (Oscillators).

The Predicted Trendline—A Projection from a Single Point of Contact

When a conventional trendline is drawn across two or more points and a parallel "channel line" is drawn on the left-hand side of

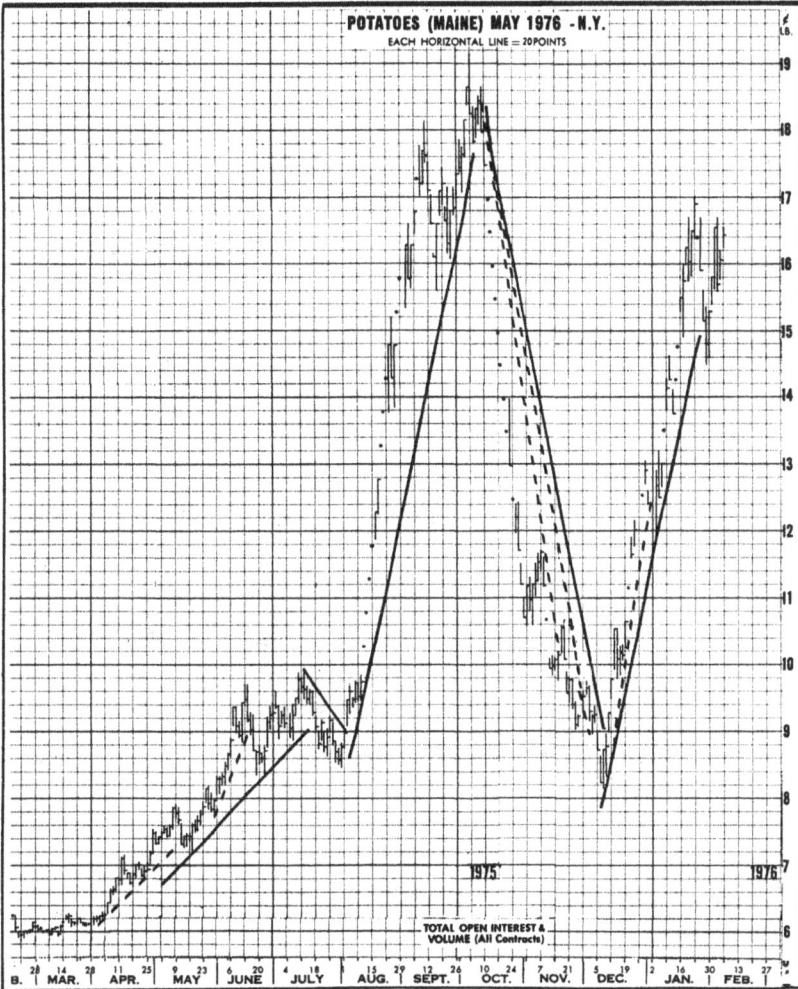

Figure 26. Conventional Trendlines: In this wild market, where prices doubled and halved and doubled again within a six-month period, trendlines were very helpful. The dotted lines show trendlines that gave false signals. Despite those whipsaws, the gains would have far outweighed the losses if trendline signals had been faithfully followed.

the trend channel, the two lines will often mark the approximate boundaries of the trend as it progresses. It stands to reason that if the "channel line" could be correctly drawn first, before the location of the trendline is known, the future trendline could then be predicted

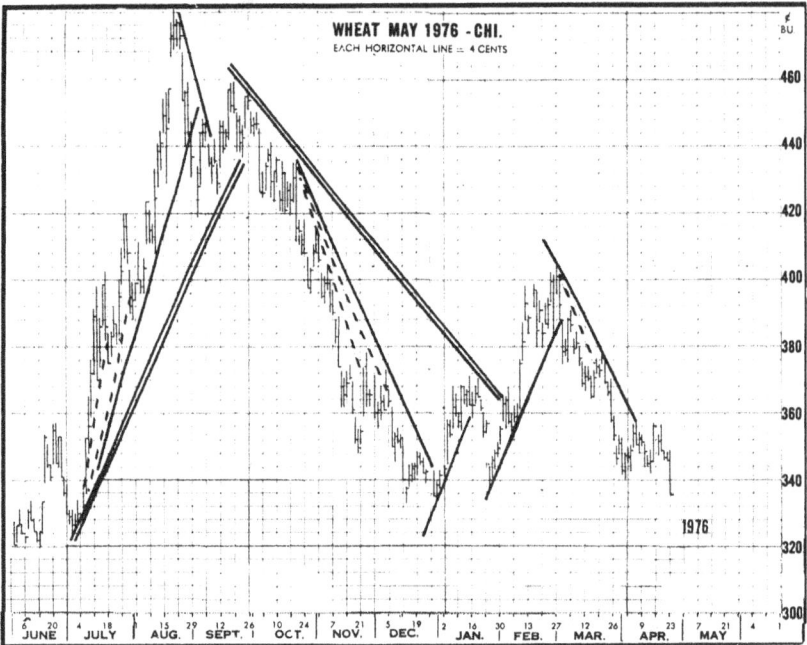

Figure 27. Conventional Trendlines: "Fan" trendlines occurred twice on this chart—during the July-August advance and the October-December decline. In each case the penetration of the third trendline proved valid. The double lines show where major trendlines could have been drawn.

by drawing it parallel to the channel line *across a single projecting point.*

There are obvious advantages in knowing in advance the approximate position of a future trendline. While this projection can sometimes be accomplished by the simple expedient of drawing a "guideline" across the "channel side" of the trend, and then drawing a trendline parallel to the guideline, I have found that there are certain variations in the technique that can enhance the probability of success.

To facilitate the explanation of this technique, only uptrends will be considered, but it is to be understood that the same procedures apply in the reverse direction in the case of downtrends. The term "channel guideline" as used here will refer to the line that is normally drawn parallel to an established trendline to form the other

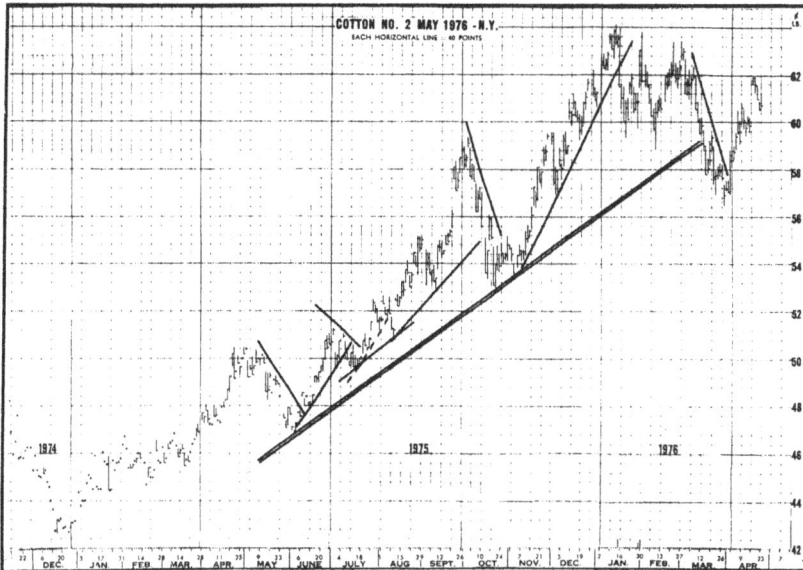

Figure 28. Conventional Trendlines: The minor trendlines drawn in the course of this prolonged advance in cotton would have amply rewarded the trader who followed them. On the other hand, the penetration of the major uptrend line (double line) eventually proved to be premature, as the March 1976 low later turned out to be the bottom of that downturn. However, a minor downtrend line across the March rallies would have given good protection.

side of the trend channel, and which is now to be drawn *first* as a guide to estimating a parallel trendline. The first fact to be noted is that, for purposes of plotting the channel guideline, the *initial* upward leg of a bull trend (or the initial downward leg of a bear trend) receives different treatment than the subsequent stages of the advance.

The Initial Predicted Trendline

In an uptrend, the initial upward leg of the new bull trend appears to have a close relationship to the final phase of the bear trend that preceded it. To find the starting point for the appropriate channel guideline of the initial upleg, it is necessary to go back to that previous downtrend. What we are looking for is the lowest point of the downleg that was completed just *before* the final bottom was made—

the next-to-the-last bottom, or "penultimate" low. In a head-and-shoulders bottom, that point would be the low of the left shoulder; in a double bottom it would be the first bottom. Closing prices are not used; only the daily high-low ranges are considered.

The channel guideline for the Initial Predicted Trendline will start at that penultimate intra-day low and will extend in a straight line (through some of the price action) to the *highest point* of the first upleg. (Of course, that highest point cannot be identified with certainty until after the subsequent downside reaction has gotten under way, but the channel guideline could be tentatively fitted to a suspected top at any time and modified later if necessary.) It should be noted that the channel guideline for the initial upleg will of necessity cut through part of the old downtrend, and might also slice through a portion of the upleg itself. Once the channel guideline has been drawn, the parallel predicted trendline will be projected

Figure 29. Initial Predicted Trendline: A guideline is first drawn through the penultimate low and the first new high (both circled). The Initial Predicted Trendline is then drawn parallel to the guideline across the outermost intraday dip (the low in this instance). The Initial Predicted Trendline acts as a rising support level that tends to stop the next downward reaction. On this chart it was touched by a reaction and became the valid conventional uptrend line.

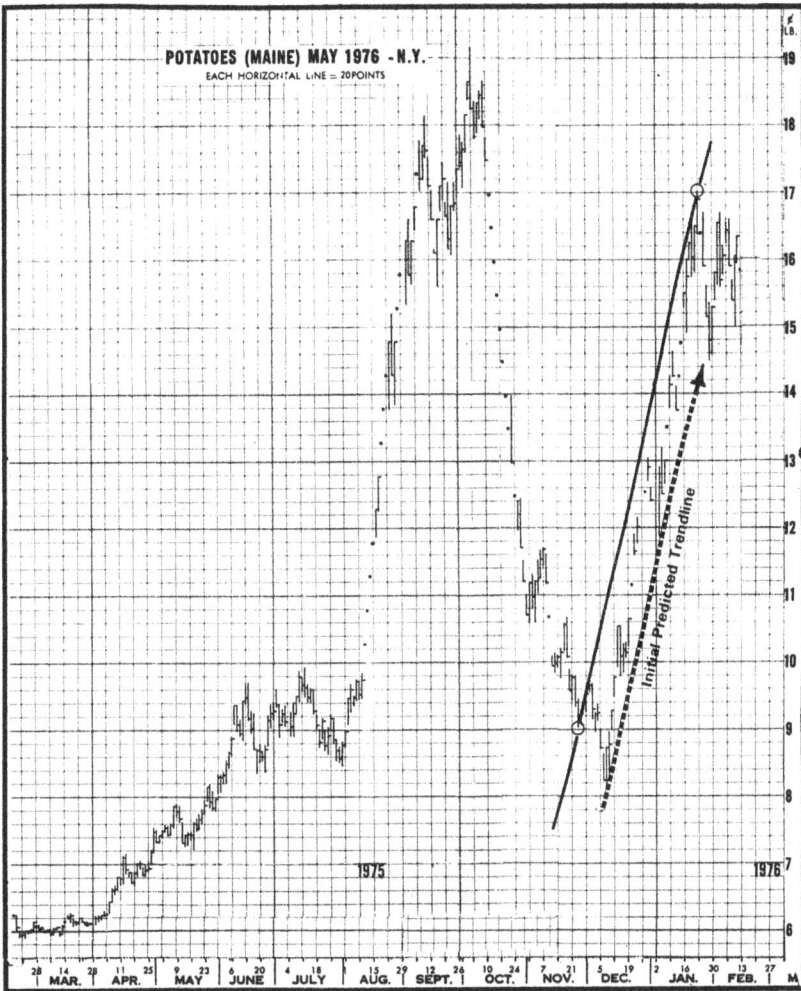

POTATOES (MAINE) MAY 1976 - N.Y.
EACH HORIZONTAL LINE = 20 POINTS

Initial Predicted Trendline

1975   1976

28 14 28 | 11 25 | 9 23 | 6 20 | 4 18 | 15 29 | 12 26 | 10 24 | 7 21 | 5 19 | 2 16 30 | 13 27 | M
MAR. | APR. | MAY | JUNE | JULY | AUG. | SEPT. | OCT. | NOV. | DEC. | JAN. | FEB. |

Figure 30. Initial Predicted Trendline: The December-January advance could be treated as the possible initial up-leg of a new uptrend (even though a second up-leg did not actually develop). The guideline on the left was drawn from the low point of the last dip before the final low, through the high of the advance. The Initial Predicted Trendline was drawn parallel to the guideline across the outermost projecting dip of the advance (which happened to be the low). The trendline acted as a rising zone of support that stopped the downward reaction in late January. After the price bounced from that support area, a valid uptrend line could be substituted for the Initial Predicted Trendline.

from a single point—the outermost intra-day low point along the uptrend. That point might be the low of the move, or it might be one of the dips along the way.

The resulting predicted trendline will then serve as a rising zone of support that should tend to halt any decline that comes down to meet it.

Examples of the Initial Predicted Trendline ("Initial PTL") are shown in the charts of March 1976 Plywood, May 1976 Maine Potatoes and June 1976 Live Hogs (figs. 29, 30 and 31).

Not all trend reversals lend themselves to this technique. If a penultimate low (or high) cannot be readily identified, or if the initial leg of the new trend is not clearly defined, it may not be possible to draw the initial channel guideline with any certainty.

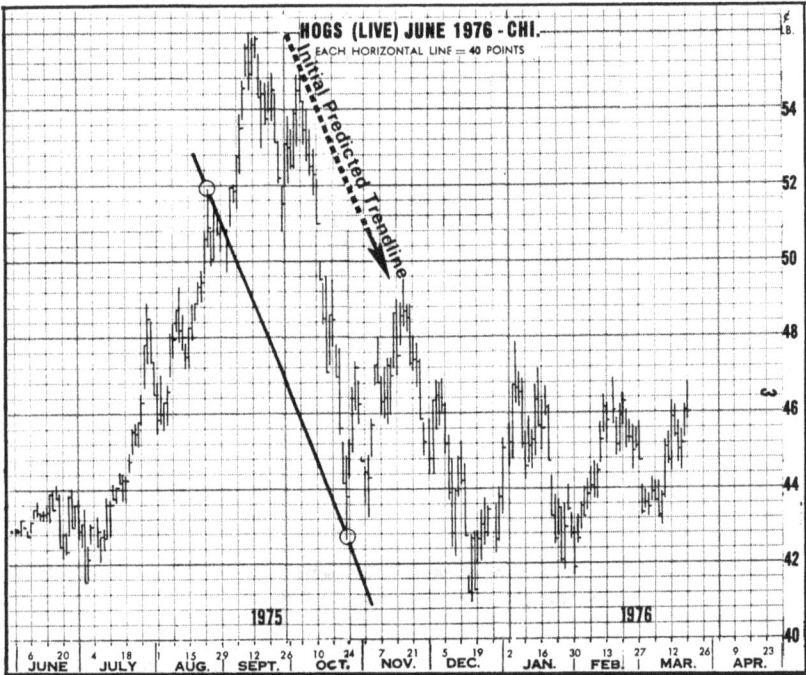

Figure 31. Initial Predicted Trendline: The guideline on the left was drawn from the penultimate high price through the lowest point of the decline. The Initial Predicted Trendline was drawn parallel to the guideline from a single point representing the outermost intra-day high in the downward move. The November rally was halted in the close vicinity of this downward line of resistance. After prices backed away, a conventional downtrend line could be drawn across the October-November peaks.

The Intermediate Predicted Trendline

After the downward correction of the initial upleg has been completed and the bull move has been resumed, it is time to watch for an Intermediate Predicted Trendline. The slope of this trendline could be approximated by placing a channel guideline across the intra-day peaks of the upward channel. However, in past tests I have

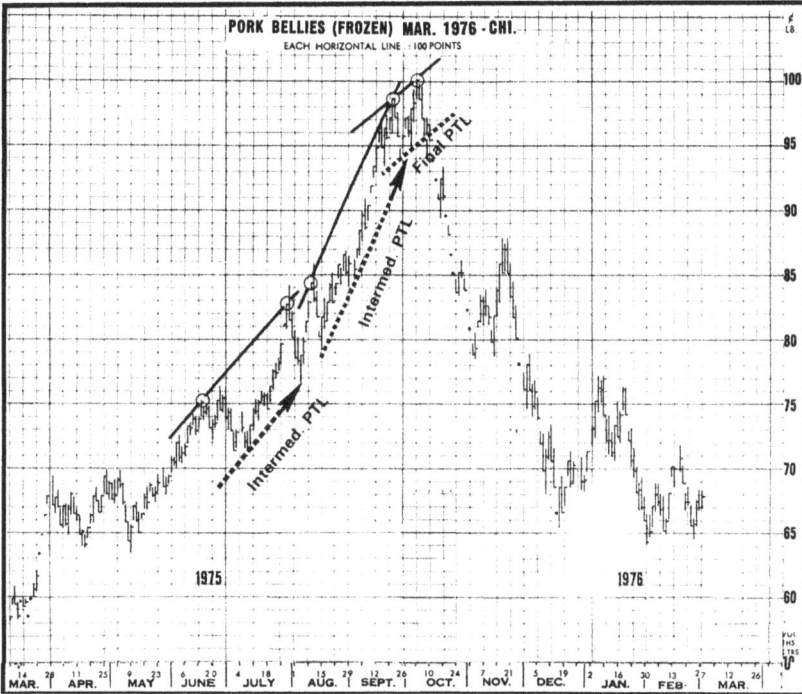

Figure 32. Intermediate and Final Predicted Trendlines: The guidelines for the Intermediate Predicted Trendlines were drawn through the outermost *closing* prices on the left side of the trend. The Predicted Trendlines were then drawn parallel to the guidelines across the outermost *intraday* reaction, and acted as a rising support zone. When the steep advance showed signs of bending over, a Final Predicted Trendline could be drawn. The guideline for the Final Predicted Trendline is drawn by the same rules that govern the Intermediate Predicted Trendline—through the outermost closing prices along the left side of the trend. The Final Predicted Trendline is then drawn parallel to the guideline, and acts not only as a line of support but also as a valid trendline whose penetration signals a reversal of trend direction. On this chart a Final Predicted Trendline might also have been tentatively drawn across the two high closings in August. However, the dip that followed would not have penetrated the line.

found that a more accurate Intermediate Predicted Trendline has usually been obtained by drawing the channel guideline through the extreme *closing prices* rather than through the intra-day highs. The Intermediate Predicted Trendline is then projected parallel to the upward channel guideline across the outermost projecting intra-day low (*not* the closing price) that lies *between the closing prices that were used for the channel guideline.* The resulting predicted trendline, as in the case of the Initial Predicted Trendline, must be considered as a rising support zone, and not as a final valid trendline.

There may be more than one intermediate upleg within the bull trend. Each new upleg can be treated in the same manner as the first intermediate upleg, with its own independent Intermediate Predicted Trendline. Some examples of Intermediate Predicted Trendlines are included in the charts of March 1976 Pork Bellies, March 1976 Soybeans, and March 1976 Soybean Oil shown in figs. 32, 33, and 34.

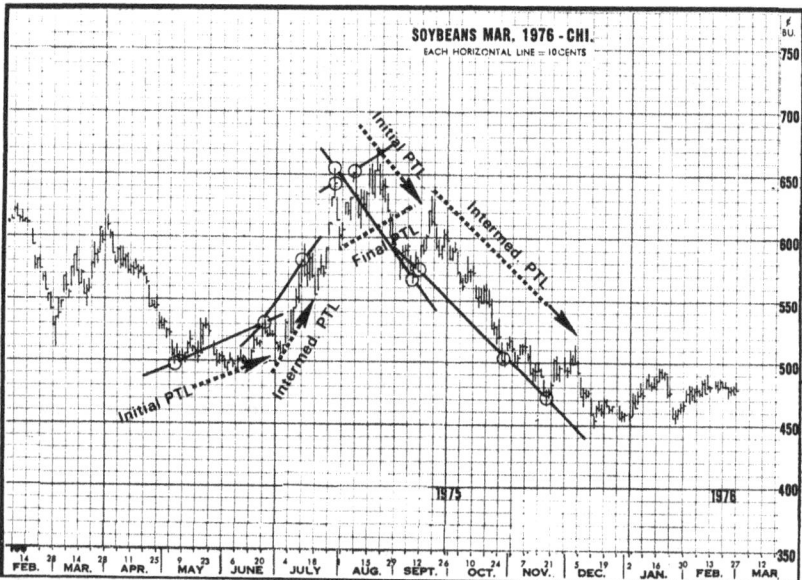

Figure 33. Initial, Intermediate, and Final Predicted Trendlines: The Initial and Intermediate Predicted Trendlines on this chart showed the rising support zone in the uptrend and the falling resistance zone in the downtrend. The Final Predicted Trendline gave a valid bear signal when penetrated.

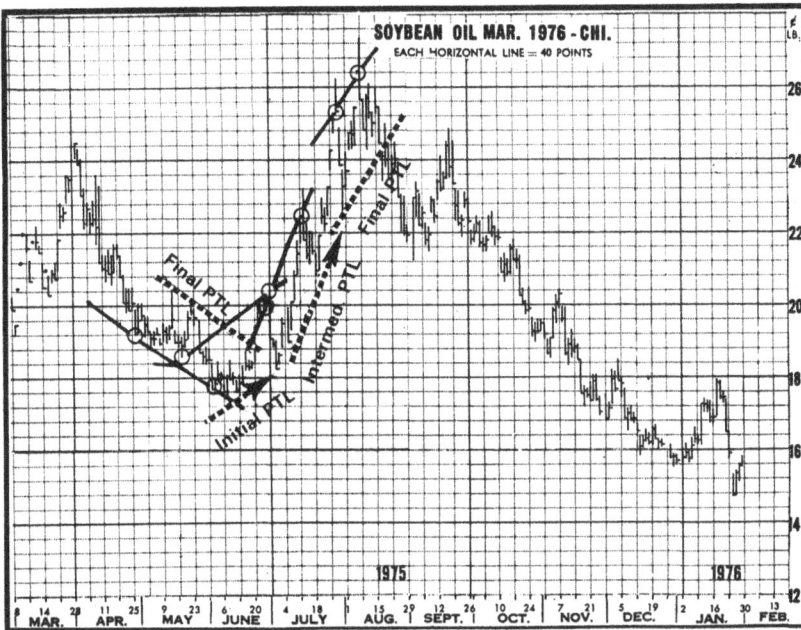

Figure 34. Initial, Intermediate, and Final Predicted Trendlines: The market action during the early life of this contract corresponded well to the forecasts of Predicted Trendlines. The upturn in June was signaled by the penetration of a Final Predicted Trendline. The dip early in July met support at a rising Initial Predicted Trendline, and the dip later that month began from a rising Intermediate Predicted Trendline. The penetration of a Final Predicted Trendline in August signaled the end of the uptrend.

The Final Predicted Trendline

Many bull and bear markets tend either to slow down and bend over in a narrow channel or to accelerate in a steep climactic finale as they get ready to reverse from one trend direction to another. In either event, a Final Predicted Trendline can be applied to the potential top formation. The slope formation described in Chapter 2 is one variation of this type of top or bottom. In a potential top formation, the Final Predicted Trendline is obtained in the same manner as the Intermediate Predicted Trendline. That is, the channel guideline for the Final Predicted Trendline is drawn through the high closing prices, and a parallel trendline is projected across the outermost dip between the high closing prices used. The Final Predicted Trendline, however, should lean either somewhat toward the horizontal or very close to the vertical. It should be noted that the Final Predicted Trendline serves a much more ambitious purpose than the Initial Predicted Trendlines. The Final Predicted Trendline is not only a rising support line, it is also to be utilized as *a precise and valid trendline whose downside penetration will signal the end of that bull trend.*

Examples of Final Predicted Trendlines are included in figs. 32, 33, and 34.

The Reaction Predicted Trendline

A trendline that is sometimes difficult to place correctly is one across the borders of a temporary reaction. The type of reaction that

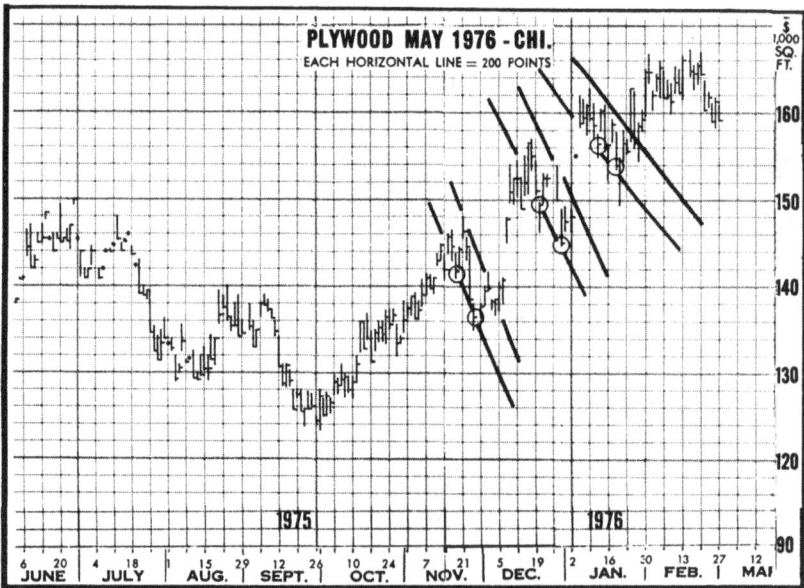

Figure 35. Reaction Predicted Trendlines: Most reactions that last about two weeks or longer respond well to this technique. The rules are identical to those for the Final Predicted Trendline. A guideline is drawn through the outermost **closing** prices on the left side of the reaction and a parallel trendline is drawn across the outermost projecting intraday point on the right side of the reaction. The penetration of that trendline signals the end of the reaction and the resumption of the main trend.

concerns us here is not the brief three or four-day move, but a reaction that continues for perhaps two weeks or longer, and may sometimes resemble a flag formation.

A downward reaction of this type (within a bull move) will usually contain two or more prominent dips, while an upward reaction (within a bear trend) will show two or more bulges. Once the reaction has been completed the primary trend is likely to be resumed, and the correct timing of the resumption of the main trend can be of considerable importance to the trader, especially if defensive measures were taken during the reaction as a precaution against a possible reversal of the main trend.

Frequently, what appears to be a correct trendline (across the tops of a downward reaction or across the lows of an upward reaction) eventually proves to be false, and the penetration of that trendline is

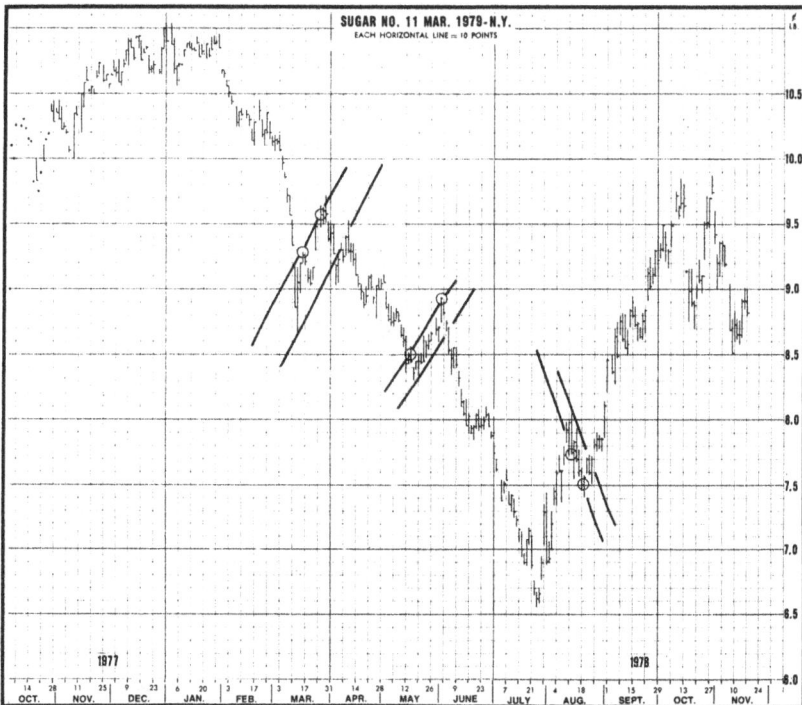

Figure 36. Reaction Predicted Trendlines: Two upward reactions and one downward reaction on this chart were of long enough duration to permit Reaction Predicted Trendlines to be drawn. In each instance the penetration of the trendline gave a valid signal of the resumption of the main trend.

then followed by a further extension of the reaction. It is usually possible to establish the correct and valid trendline of a reaction by following a procedure similar to that used in obtaining a Final Predicted Trendline.

In a downward reaction (within a bull trend), a channel guideline is drawn through the outermost *closing prices* of two or more dips, and a parallel downtrend line is projected across the outermost intra-day high of the downward reaction.

That downtrend line across the reaction is to serve as the precise and valid trendline whose penetration will signal the end of the reaction.

Sometimes that parallel trendline will happen to coincide exactly with a conventional downtrend line that would normally be drawn across two or more peaks. But as often as not the parallel downtrend line will be suspended from the single point of contact used to draw it. That single outermost point might be the recent high of the move where the reaction began, or it might be one of the bulges on the way down.

Upward reactions in a bear market would be treated in the same manner, using an upward channel guideline through closing prices and a parallel Reaction Predicted Trendline.

Examples of Reaction Predicted Trendlines are shown in the charts of May 1976 Plywood and March 1979 Sugar #11, figs. 35 and 36.

A special application of the trendline concept is the *curved* trend channel, which is discussed in the next chapter.

CHAPTER 4

Curved Trend Channels

Value of Curved Channels

In Chapter 2 the importance of identifying the minor, major, and longer term trends was stressed. It is essential for the chartist to keep in mind at all times which trend he is trading, and to have some means of differentiating between counterswings *within* the trading trend and counterswings that *break* the trading trend. Furthermore, an understanding of the changing relationship between the smaller trends and the larger trends can be helpful in projecting future trends. These important objectives can usually be achieved through the use of specially constructed curved channels.

While commodity futures often move in fairly well-defined trend channels whose boundaries can be marked off with straight lines, a smoother and more revealing chart picture is frequently obtained if curved lines are fitted to the trend channels. Examples of such trend channels are shown in figs. 37 and 38 superimposed on charts of December 1978 Corn and March 1976 Plywood.

Characteristics of Curved Channels

Empirical tests made by the author on charts of many different commodities indicate that the proper curved channels have certain characteristics. The two most important characteristics are:

1. Each trend channel tends to maintain a constant *vertical* width throughout the life of the contract.
2. The vertical widths of different-sized curved trend channels on a commodity futures chart increase in size geometrically; that is, the vertical width of each channel is approximately double the width of the next smaller channel.

In the Corn chart (fig. 37), it can be seen that the constant vertical widths of the three channels shown are 8¢, 16¢ and 32¢. In the Plywood chart (fig. 38), they are $8.00, $16.00, and $32.00. In both charts, one additional smaller curved channel could have been constructed at about half the vertical width of the smallest one shown. However, the smallest of the three channels shown corresponds to what would generally be accepted as the "minor" trend.

Another characteristic of curved trend channels is the tendency for

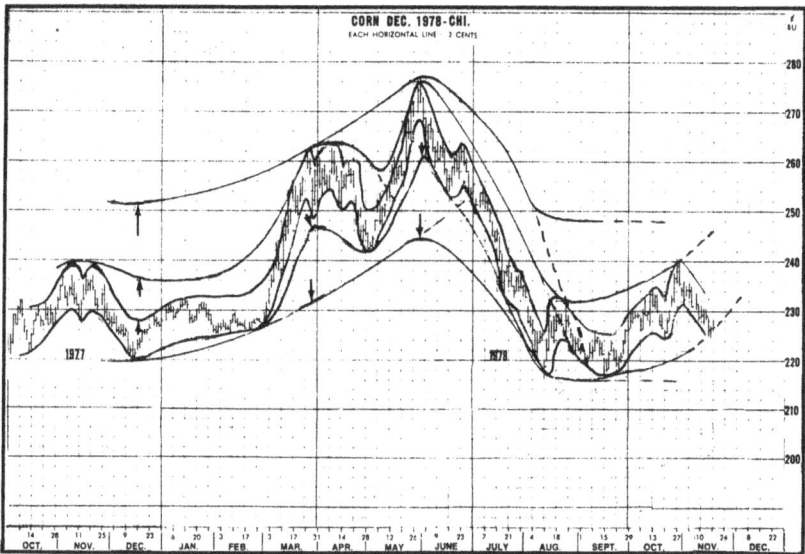

Figure 37. Curved Channels Showing Geometrical Progression of Channel Widths: Commodity futures prices tend to move within curved channels of fixed vertical width. Each channel is double the vertical width of the next smaller one. On this chart the channels are 8¢, 16¢ and 32¢ wide. The channels help to identify the minor, major, and long-term trends. As each trend progresses the channels can be projected slightly ahead as a guide to future support and resistance areas and to warn of a change in trend direction.

the vertical width of the minor trend channels to range, with few exceptions, between 4% and 6% of the prevailing price level of that commodity. Listed below are the vertical channel widths of the minor, major and long term trends that were found to fit most 1978 delivery months in the commodities named. Also shown is the approximate percentage size of the minor trend channel in each case.

CURVED CHANNEL SIZES—1978 DELIVERY MONTHS

Commodity	Minor, Major, Long Term	Approx. percent (Minor)
Cattle	2.00¢, 4.00¢, 8.00¢	4%
Cocoa	8.00¢, 16.00¢, 32.00¢	5%
Coffee	10.00¢, 20.00¢, 40.00¢	5%
Copper	3.00¢, 6.00¢, 12.00¢	5%
Corn	8¢, 16¢, 32¢	3½%
Cotton	3.00¢, 6.00¢, 12.00¢	5%
Gold (Comex)	$10.00, $20.00, $40.00	6%
Hogs	2.00¢, 4.00¢, 8.00¢	5%
Lumber	$10.00, $20.00, $40.00	5%
Oats	6¢, 12¢, 24¢	4½%
Fzn. Orange Juice	10.00¢, 20.00¢, 40.00¢	10%
Platinum	$12.50, $25.00, $50.00	6¼%
Plywood	$10.00, $20.00, $40.00	5%
Pork Bellies	5.00¢, 10.00¢, 20.00¢	7½%
Potatoes (N.Y. Merc.)	0.50¢, 1.00¢, 2.00¢	6½%
Rapeseed (Wpg.)	$10.00, $20.00, $40.00	3½%
Silver (N.Y. and Chgo.)	20.00¢, 40.00¢, 80.00¢	4%
Soybeans	40¢, 80¢, $1.60	6%
Soybean Meal	$9.00, $18.00, $36.00	5%
Soybean Oil	1.00¢, 2.00¢, 4.00¢	5%
Sugar #11	0.50¢, 1.00¢, 2.00¢	4½%
Wheat (CBT)	15¢, 30¢, 60¢	5%

A question that naturally arises is: What happens, then, when a commodity price moves up rapidly, perhaps doubling in value in a relatively short time? Does the vertical width of each channel remain the same? The answer to this question reveals another remarkable characteristic I have observed in curved channels. When a bull trend accelerates and prices climb rapidly to a much higher level, *each trend—minor, major and long-term—leaps into the next larger channel,* double the vertical width of the old channel. Likewise, when a bear market has a sudden substantial decline, each trend sinks into the

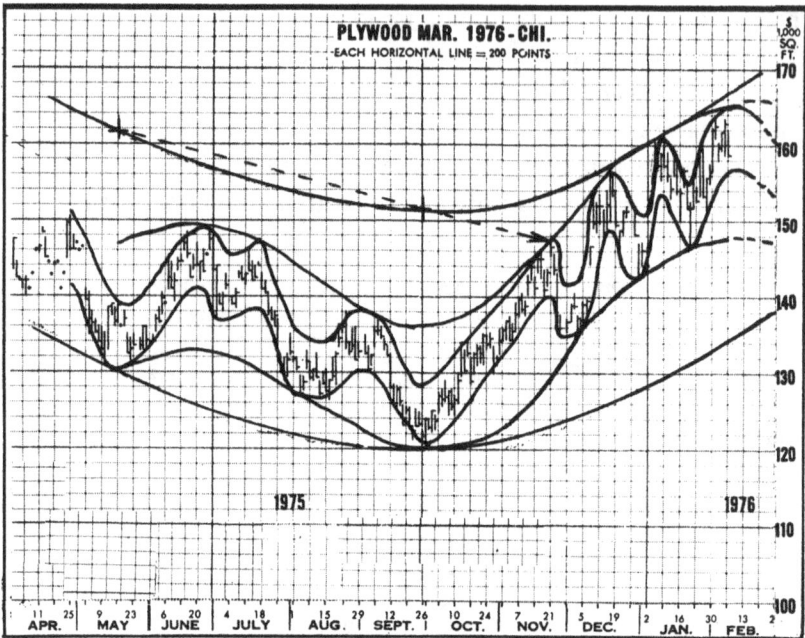

Figure 38. Curved Channels Showing Geometrical Progression of Channel Widths: On this chart the channels have vertical widths of $8, $16 and $32. By projecting each channel slightly ahead, changes in the minor, major and long-term trends can be identified.

next smaller channel. This change of channels is not a gradual process; it happens suddenly in the course of a rapid move.

The correct channel sizes of a particular commodity contract can be determined only by trial and error. The 4 to 6% range for the minor trend can be used as a guide. If two or three typical price swings can be found and a straight line drawn across two outermost points on the left-hand or "channel" side of each swing, the vertical height from the channel line to the outermost reaction on the trendline side of the channel can be used as a guide to the correct width of that channel. Also, if a horizontal trading range can be found, its vertical height will usually equal the vertical width of one of the channels, since trading ranges often fit precisely into a curved channel that is temporarily moving sideways or is slowly bending around. Once the vertical width of any one channel has been deter-

mined to the chartist's satisfaction, all larger and small curved channels can be estimated by simply doubling or halving the vertical
width of the known channel.

When drawing the curved channels in an uptrend, the upper line
of the channel should generally hug the peaks, and the lower line of
the upward channel should be plotted by projecting the channel
width downward from the upper line. In a downtrend, it is assumed
that prices will tend to run along the lower line of the channel, with
the upper line a measured distance above. In any event, the channel
should be drawn so as to include all the swings within that trend. If
the price appears to project beyond the channel width, the channel
must be bent to include that action.

How Curved Channels Identify the Trend

Curved channels can serve the chartist in a number of ways. Of
greatest importance, perhaps, is their use in identifying trends. In the
examples shown in figs. 37 and 38, as already indicated, the smallest
of the three channels encloses the erratic minor trend, while the two
larger channels enclose what might be called the major and long-
term trends. As market action progresses, each channel can be projected slightly ahead in its prevailing direction. The market itself will
quickly show whether a trend channel is bending around and reversing direction. The succession of ascending or descending tops
and bottoms is clearly defined in each trend by the change in direction of the corresponding channel. There is therefore little room
for doubt as to the direction of the minor, major, and long-term
trends at any point in time once the curved channels are determined
and kept current.

How Curved Channels Show Support and
Resistance Areas

A second important function of curved channels is to establish
approximate support and resistance levels. As mentioned above, the
constant vertical width of the channels enables the chartist to project

each channel a short distance ahead. Since each trend channel moves within the boundaries of the next larger channel, the larger channel tends to stop the progress of the smaller trend.

For example, in the chart of March 1976 Plywood (fig. 38), when the minor trend turned up in late August the resistance around the $138 level was indicated by the descending major curved trendline. Since the major channel is approximately 1600 points wide, the upper line had to be around $143 in the first week of August and around $138 by the first week of September.

A similar downward projection of the lower line of that second channel would imply support around the $118–120 level at the end of September. In mid-October, resistance around $135 coincided with a tentative projection of the upper line of the second channel, and the market did stop there for a while before turning up. The subsequent upturn through the $136 level (1600 points above the $120 low) turned the major trend channel up. The three big dips during December and January also fitted well within the 1600-point channel, and could be projected as support levels within the major curved upward channel.

Similar measurements in the smaller and larger channels could project short-term and long-term support and resistance levels. To cite one example: The upper channel line of the largest channel as it declined, by the rule of geometric progression, had to be about $32.00 above the May low (near the beginning of the contract) and $32.00 above the contract low made in late September. At the end of September, a downward projection of that long-term upper channel line would have met the October-November advance head-on at its very peak. Until that November peak was exceeded, the long-term channel was still pointing downward.

Mathematical Simulation of the Curved Trend Channels

Although the construction of curved channels is largely a matter of personal judgment, it is possible to approximate the correct channels mathematically by using a specially constructed set of moving averages. While the curved channels normally have a constant vertical width, the mathematically constructed channels use a con-

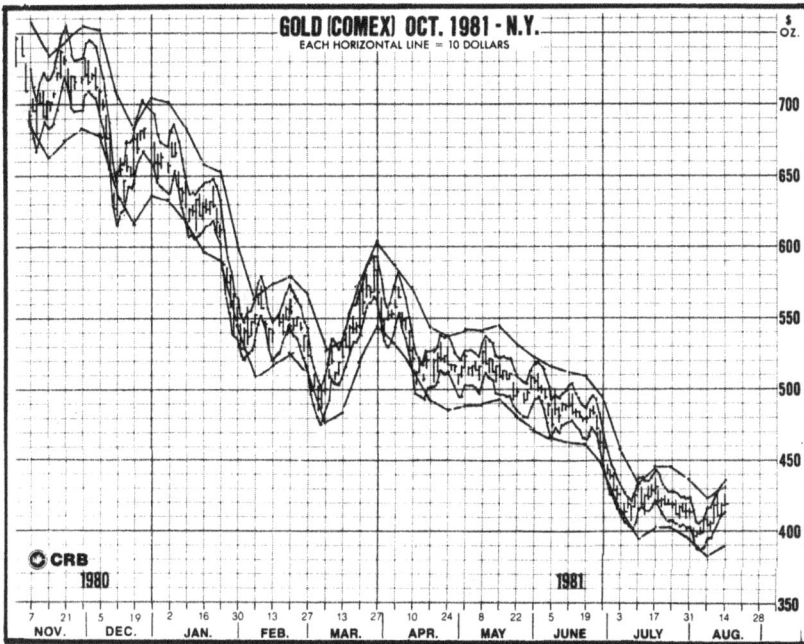

Figure 38a. An Example of Mathematically Simulated Curved Trend Channels.
The 5% and 10% channels shown here were made by projecting weighted moving averages through the center of the 5-day and 3-week trends as described in the text.

stant *percentage* width. The first step is to construct a moving average that will tend to run through the center of the channel. There is more than one way to accomplish this, but the method described below will be found to be relatively simple and effective. Once the correct centered moving average has been calculated, one can proceed on the assumption that most minor trend channels tend to have a vertical width of about 5% of the price. The next larger channel usually runs about 10% of the price. We will not concern ourselves here with the third channel (the 20% channel) as the first two channels will usually serve the purposes of most commodity traders. Once the correct channels have been plotted mathematically on the charts it should be possible to adapt them to one's trading procedures and perhaps utilize them as the basis for an automatic trading method.

The Minor Trend Channel

The centered moving average that we construct for the minor trend must not only run through the approximate center of the channel, it must also be projected to the present day if we are to use it effectively. This can be accomplished with a "least squares trendline." If your calculator is not programmed for linear regression you can use a special simple weighted moving average to solve any point on the least squares trendline. To obtain a centered moving average for the minor trend we will use a five-day series of prices. We will use the average daily price based on the high plus low, divided by two. (Disregard the closing price.) Using that average daily price, we want to project a least squares trendline through the five-day series and obtain the value of that line on the fifth day. The weighted average procedure is as follows.

Multiply the average price on
Day #1 by −.2
Day #2 by   0
Day #3 by +.2
Day #4 by +.4
Day #5 by +.6
The sum equals the price of the centered moving average on Day #5.

The answer will be exactly the same as the answer you would get on a programmed calculator when you solve for $5Y_4$. Now that we have the centered moving average for Day #5, all we have to do is add 2½ % to that price to obtain the high point of the channel, and subtract 2½ % from the price to obtain the low point of the channel. You plot those high and low points on that same fifth day on the chart. Repeat that process the next day and the next, etc., and in most commodity markets you will see a reasonably correct minor trend curved channel take shape. Although that 5% channel will enclose the minor trend of most markets satisfactorily you will probably find that the reversal signals are a little too slow for actual trading purposes. If you would like to use the upper and lower channel lines as stop-loss points for trading purposes, reduce the 5% channel to 3%, by adding or subtracting 1½% from the centered moving average. That tighter channel can be used as a boundary line for signaling a reversal of the minor trend. Some volatile commodities might require 2% plus and minus, some markets might give better results at 1¼%. The best percentage to use could be determined by some preliminary tests at a few critical turning points.

The Major Trend Channel

For most trading purposes, the "major trend" can be considered as the second channel, the one that tends to run about 10% of the price in vertical width. To obtain a centered moving average for that channel we will use a three-week series of prices, on a weekly basis. We find the average price of the week by adding the weekly high plus the weekly low and dividing the sum by two. Using those average weekly prices we must project a least squares trendline through the three-week series to the third week. (On a programmed calculator that point is $3Y_2$.) The weighted average formula for this employs some endless decimals, but four or five decimal places should insure ample accuracy.

> Multiply the average price of
> Week #1 by −.16667
> Week #2 by +.33333
> Week #3 by +.83333
> The sum equals the centered moving average price at week #3.

To simulate the high and low lines of the major curved channel, we add 5% and subtract 5% from the centered moving average price. We then plot those high and low points on the Friday of that third week. At the end of the following week we repeat the procedure for the latest three-week period and plot the high and low points on that Friday's line. We then connect the Friday points with a straight line to simulate the major curved channel. Figure 38a shows both the major and minor trend channels as calculated for the October 1981 gold contract.

For trading purposes, however, we will want to tighten up those channel lines, as we did in the minor trend channel. For most commodities plus and minus 3% will do the trick. Use the price of that channel point for the entire next week (as a horizontal line on the chart). In a major uptrend you use the lower line as the borderline for signaling a downturn; in a major downtrend you use the upper line. As in the case of the minor trend, the major channel lines in some markets might need a slightly larger or slightly smaller percentage distance from the centered moving average price. A little preliminary testing at some critical turning points should help to determine the percentage that is likely to prove the best.

So far, we have been primarily concerned with projecting trend direction. Now let's look at some techniques designed to project price objectives.

CHAPTER 5

Predicting How Far a Move Will Go

One Dozen Methods of Projecting Price Objectives

Although the primary function of price-chart analysis is to determine the direction of large and small trends, the daily price movements of a commodity futures contract will often follow some characteristic pattern that will enable the chartist to project one or more price objectives. In many such instances there will be more than one measuring method that can be applied. When two or more measurements cluster around the same price level, the probability of that level being reached is enhanced. The principle of looking for two or more measurements that agree is consistent with the Rule of Multiple Techniques described in Chapter 1.

As accurate as many projections may prove to be, a price move may sometimes either turn back before reaching the objective or continue far beyond it. *The projection of upside and downside objectives, therefore, must always be viewed as a supplementary technique that is subordinate to basic trend analysis.* The value of a measured objective lies in its ability to give the chart trader a means of estimating the potential of a particular price move, and serves as a warning to him to be on the alert for signs of a possible price reaction or trend reversal in that area.

Some of the methods for projecting price objectives have already been mentioned in the preceding chapters. Of the 12 methods to be described here, six are probably well known to most chartists. These are: (1) support and resistance levels; (2) the head-and-shoulders measurement; (3) the triangle measurement; (4) the swing measurement; (5) the 50% reaction; and, (6) the midway gap measurement. One method, the Rule of Seven, came briefly to my attention many years ago, but appears to be unknown to most chartists. The remaining five techniques are based purely on my own observations and research over the years. These are: (1) the counter-swing measurement; (2) the slope formation measurement; (3) the predicted trendline measurement; (4) the curved trend channel objective; and, (5) the 17-35 measurement.

Price Support and Resistance Levels

One form that a support or resistance level takes is a prominent previous low or high price. If the market declines and approaches a price level where strong demand previously was able to turn the price up, the decline is likely to meet support again around that same price level. In an advancing market, if the price rises to a level where selling was previously in evidence, the advance is likely to encounter resistance there again.

Another form of price support or resistance is the congestion area. A rising market that has little or no overhanging resistance to block it is likely to continue moving up as long as there is "clear sailing," or until it reaches a resistance level. If that resistance is in the form of a congestion area—an area where prices previously stabilized for several days or weeks—the upside price objectives will be somewhere between the high and the low of that congestion area.

It is important to make a distinction between support and resistance levels that are a potential *obstacle* to a move that *might* get under way, and those that are potential *objectives* in a move that is *already* under way. Only when the price has broken out of some type of formation or trend pattern and a trend has been indicated in the direction of the objective can one consider utilizing a distant support or resistance level as an objective.

Head-and-Shoulders Measurement

A price objective projected from a head-and-shoulders top or bottom will usually prove to be a *minimum* objective. When a head-and-shoulders appears to be forming, a trendline should be drawn across the two "armpits," thus forming the "neckline." After the right shoulder has been fully formed by a penetration of the neckline on the close, the formation will be completed and the minimum objectives can be measured. In a head-and-shoulders top, the minimum downside objective is obtained by extending a *vertical* line from the peak of the head to the sloping neckline, and then measuring that same distance downward from the point of intersection of that vertical line and the neckline. In a head-and-shoulders bottom, the same procedure is followed in the opposite direction.

An example of this measurement can be seen in fig. 5 (February 1976 Live Cattle). The vertical distance from the top of the head to the neckline (about 300 points) projects a minimum downside objective of 40.50¢, which was clearly met and exceeded. In fig. 8 (November 1975 Soybeans) the upside projection gives a minimum objective of about $5.70, which was easily realized on the initial advance.

The Triangle Measurement

Triangles that are well-defined—that contain at least two distinct rallies and two distinct dips that serve as points of contact for the converging trendlines—can be utilized for projecting minimum short-term objectives. The projection is made after the price has emerged from the triangle, thus signaling the likely direction of the next move, and is equal to the "height" of the triangle. The height of the triangle is determined by projecting a vertical line from the

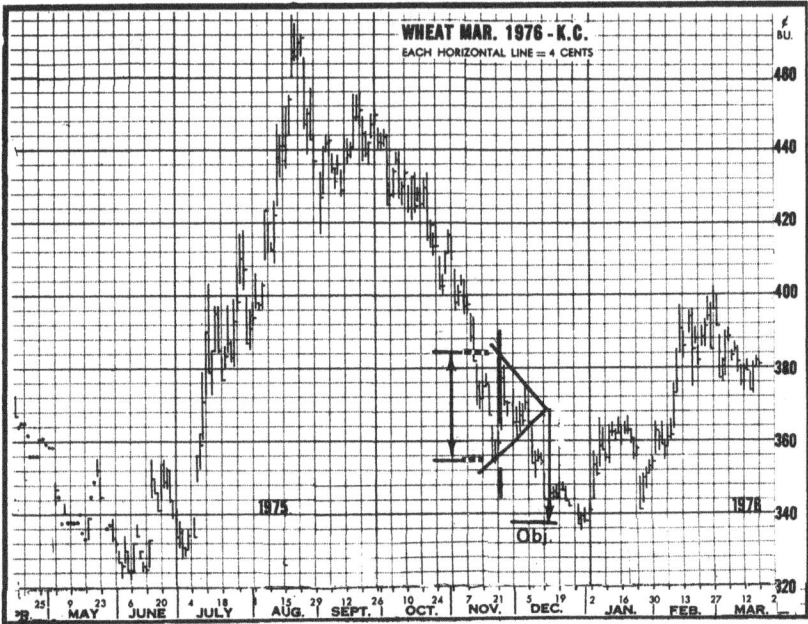

Figure 39. Triangle Measurement: Converging trendlines could be drawn across the highs and lows of the November-December price action, making a Triangle Formation. The downside penetration of the lower line signaled the resumption of the downtrend. The vertical height of the triangle projected downward from the apex gave a very accurate target price.

first point of contact on the left until it intersects the opposite trendline. That measurement is then projected from the apex of the triangle (the point of convergence of the two trendlines) in the direction of the breakout to indicate the price objective.

Looking back at fig. 6 (February 1976 Live Cattle), the downside projection of the vertical side of the triangle from the apex gives an objective of about 40.60¢, which was reached and exceeded. In fig. 39 (March 1976 K.C. Wheat), the triangle that took shape in November and early December was eventually broken on the downside and projected a low that clearly approximated the actual bottom.

A very prolonged major triangle appears in fig. 40 (April 1976 Platinum). Although prices weaved back and forth within the formation, the important highs and lows of the converging triangle are quite clearly defined. The upside breakout gave a projection of about $183, which was at about the middle of the double-top formation.

Figure 40. Triangle Measurement: Prices weaved back and forth for several months before finally taking shape as a prolonged triangle. Although the large base seemed capable of propelling prices to much higher levels, the advance halted after satisfying the measured objective of the triangle.

The Swing Measurement

Certain types of chart formations often mark the halfway point in a price move, enabling the chartist to project an objective by means of the swing measurement. The swing measurement is based on the assumption that the next price swing in the direction of the main trend will be approximately equal in magnitude to the previous price swing in that direction. The effectiveness of this technique is largely limited to situations in which a relatively steep and rapid price move is followed by a corrective pause in the form of a triangle, flag, consolidation, or other tight formation. After the corrective pause has been completed and the original trend has been resumed, the objective is determined by measuring the extent of the previous swing and projecting that same measurement ahead from the extreme point of the reaction.

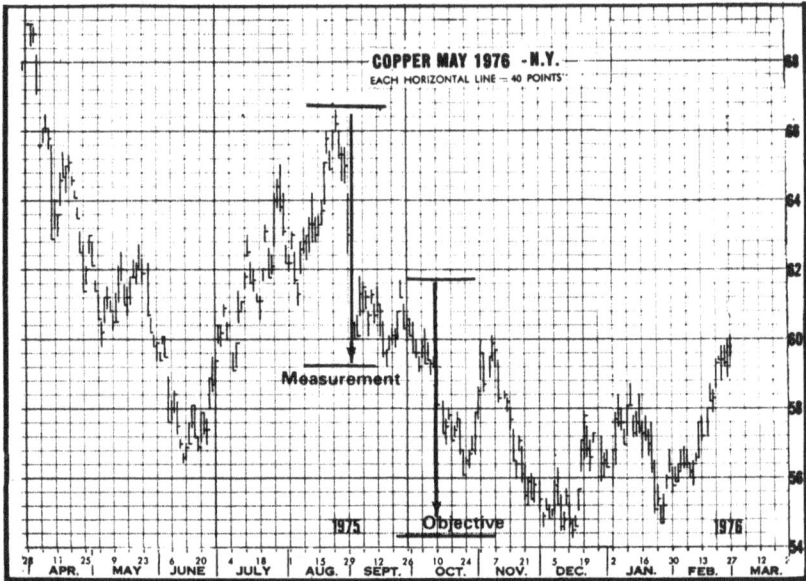

Figure 41. Swing Measurement: Price trends often contain successive price swings of equal magnitude. The second downward leg was interrupted by a sharp rally at the end of October before reaching the Swing objective. Still, the bottom that was made in December was right on target.

An example of this measurement can be seen in the chart of May 1976 Copper in fig. 41. The steep decline from the August peak of 66.60¢ to the September low of 59.20¢ was 740 points. Projecting this downward from the reaction high of 61.70¢ gave a downside objective of 54.30¢. Although a subsequent big rally temporarily interrupted the decline on its way to the objective, the bear trend eventually bottomed at 54.20¢, resulting in an unusually accurate measured objective.

The Counter-Swing Measurement

When the market is in an uptrend, if a reversal of trend begins directly from a new high (rather than from a lower top) and subsequently breaks the low of the previous dip, the price swing will often carry the same distance beneath that previous low that it went above the previous high. The same principle holds true in a downtrend that reverses from a new low and then breaks the previous high. The counter-swing measurement can also be applied to a false breakout from a consolidation. If, after breaking out on one side of a consolidation, the price reverses and goes through the other side, it will usually proceed the same distance in the new direction as it did on the false breakout.

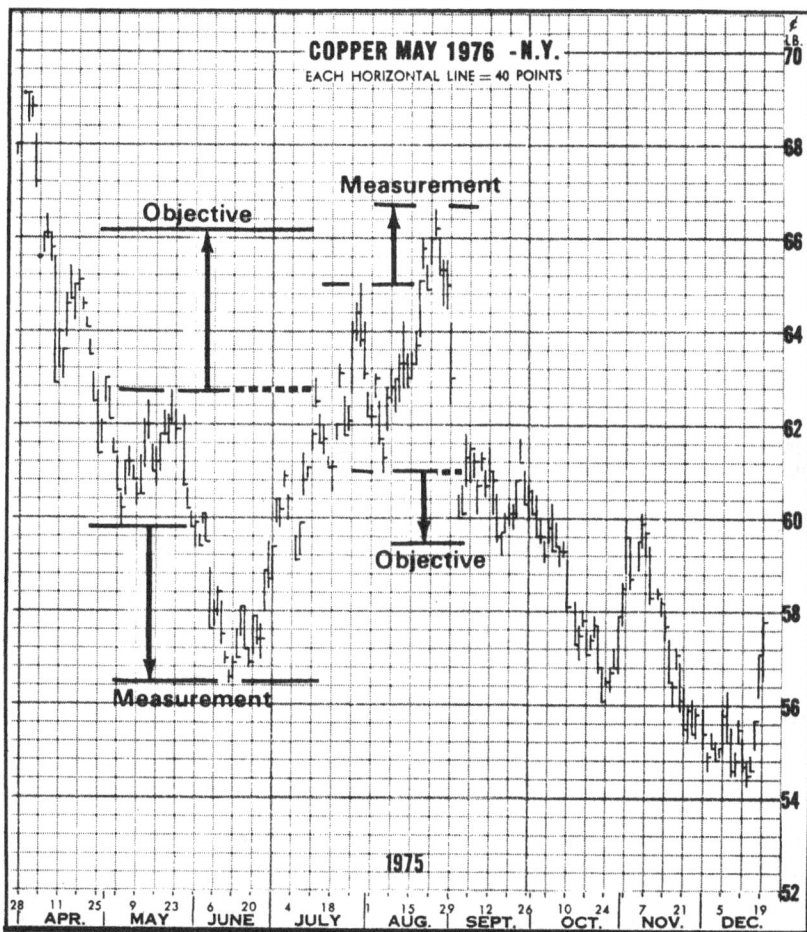

COPPER MAY 1976 - N.Y.
EACH HORIZONTAL LINE = 40 POINTS

Figure 42. Counter-Swing Measurement: When a price trend reverses from a new low or a new high and cuts through a congestion area, the price swing will often extend about the same distance on both sides of the congestion area. On this chart, when the upturn from the June low cut through the high of late May, an upside target could be projected to about the 66¢ level. The steep decline from the August high penetrated the August low, but found temporary support at about the same distance beneath that low as the distance it had previously gone above the July high.

Figure 43. Counter-Swing Measurement: The upswing from the September low met strong resistance at about the same distance above the August high as the distance it had previously fallen below the August low.

Two examples of a counter-swing can be seen in the charts of May 1976 Copper (fig. 42) and May 1976 Plywood (fig. 43). Formations of this type seem to occur quite frequently, and the measurement usually proves to be quite reliable.

The Fifty-Percent Retracement

As the name implies, this measuring device is limited to corrective price swings. It is a well-known phenomenon that occurs in the course of small, medium, and large price movements. When a price movement is interrupted by a correction, the corrective swing usually retraces about half of the move. *The halfway retracement is rarely an exact 50% measurement, but will usually fit within the limits of a 40 to 60% retracement.* Moves of major magnitude sometimes prove to be corrective reactions within a longer term trend, in which case the 50% reaction measurement provides one of the clues to the major objective.

Examples of the 50% reaction can be seen in some of the charts already shown. In fig. 11 the low of the double-top formation re-traced 41% of the June-July advance. In fig. 14 the October-December advance retraced 46½% of the bear trend. In fig. 18 the July-August decline retraced 60% of the June-July advance. In fig. 29 the August-September rally retraced 48% of the July-August decline, and the late November dip retraced 47% of the October-November advance.

Midway Gaps

It is relatively easy to distinguish midway gaps from breakaway and common gaps, but they can sometimes be confused with ex-haustion gaps. If the gap area occurs at a level where there is little or no reason to expect a climax, the gap can be assumed to be of the midway type. As the name implies, midway gaps mark the probable halfway point of a price move.

Two examples appear in the charts already shown. In fig. 8, after the upside objective of the head-and-shoulders bottom was achieved and the corrective pause completed, the upside gap in late July marked the approximate halfway point to the August peak. In fig. 18 there were several upside gaps during the July advance, but the gap that carried the advance up through the May congestion area was the important midway gap. It projected an upside objective of about 55.20¢, just a little short of the July peak.

The Slope Formation Measurement

The slope formation was described in detail in Chapter 2, and a description of its measuring capacity was included. The slope forma-tion is usually a reversal pattern, and a breakout of the formation that reverses the trend will usually carry beyond the beginning of the slope and as far as the next support or resistance level. In this capac-ity, its measuring function actually overlaps the function of support and resistance areas. In some instances the slope formation serves as a continuation pattern. When that occurs, the slope formation marks the halfway level of the price move, and its measuring function is identical to that of the swing measurement.

Predicted Trendline Measurements

This technique was covered in Chapter 3. To recap, the Initial Predicted Trendline and the Intermediate Predicted Trendline serve primarily as moving support or resistance levels that can be used as approximate objectives. The objective area moves along an ascending or descending line, depending on the direction of the predicted trendline.

The Final Predicted Trendline and the Reaction Predicted Trendline also provide objective measurements, but must be employed with caution because the penetration of those lines signals a change of trend direction.

The Curved Trend Channel Objective

This technique was described in Chapter 4 in the section entitled "How Curved Channels Show Support and Resistance Areas." There is nothing more to add to that explanation, and the listing of this method is included here merely as a reminder that it is one of the 12 recommended measuring methods.

The Rule of Seven

There appears to be no rhyme nor reason to the Rule of Seven, but it is often surprisingly accurate in its predictions. It is based on the assumption that the initial leg of a new price trend reflects the potential power of the changing forces of supply and demand sufficiently to serve as a guide to the probable extent of the price move. Put another way, using the Rule of Seven, a measurement of the initial leg of the trend is all the information needed to project one or more objectives in the direction of the new trend.

Numerous tests that I have made over the years have revealed that the formula for measuring *upside* objectives by the Rule of Seven must be varied slightly when applied to *downside* objectives. I have also observed some special characteristics of the Rule of Seven under varying trend conditions, which will be described here.

In an uptrend the basic formula is: Measure the size of the initial up-leg by subtracting the low price from the high; multiply that figure by seven; then divide that product by four to get the distance from the low to the first objective, divide the product by three for the second objective, and by two for the third objective. *Note that for each of the three objectives the respective distance figure is added to the low.*

The formula can be simplified as follows:

Upside objective #1: High minus low, multiply by 1.75, add to low price.

Upside objective #2: High minus low, multiply by 2.33, add to low price.

Upside objective #3: High minus low, multiply by 3.50, add to low price.

In a downtrend the formula is moved back one notch. The three downside objectives are obtained by multiplying the size of the initial down-leg by 7/5, 7/4, and 7/3, or 1.40, 1.75, and 2.33 respectively, and subtracting the result from the high.

One of the special characteristics I have observed is that in a measurement of the *minor trend,* the first and second objectives are often ignored by the market, and the third objective is generally reached without any significant pause along the way. A minor-trend measurement might be defined as one in which the initial leg of the new trend is completed within about six days, and might even be as brief as one or two days. In a *major trend* measurement, when the initial leg takes weeks or perhaps months to be completed, the first objective is usually the valid target.

A second characteristic I have observed is that if a *major* move continues much beyond the first objective without correcting, it is likely to stop at the second objective. As a rule of thumb, the greater the magnitude of the trend, the more likely it is to stop at the first objective, while trends of small magnitude are likely to skip the first objective and sometimes the second as well.

A third characteristic is that in dynamic markets a fourth objective must be considered. In an uptrend, the fourth objective is seven times the initial leg projected upward from the low of that leg. In a downtrend it will be 3.50 times the first leg projected downward from the high.

As with all objective measurements, the projections of the Rule of Seven are given greater weight if they coincide approximately with one or more other objective measurements.

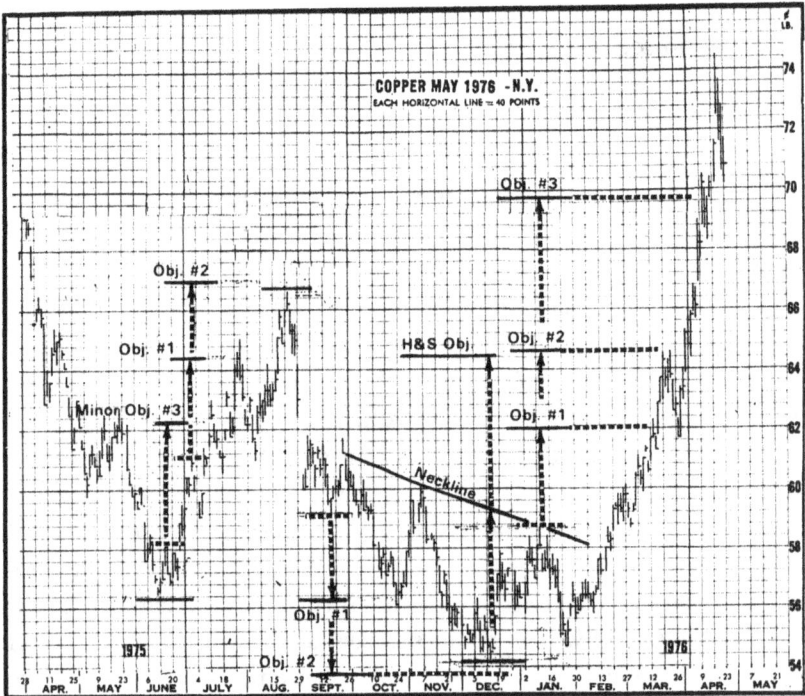

Figure 44. Rule of Seven and Head-and-shoulders Measurements: Rule of Seven projections are based on the assumption that the size of the initial leg of a new price trend is the key to the trend's potential power in the new direction. Using the Rule of Seven formula, several first, second, and third objective measurements are shown here. Note that the Head-and-Shoulders measurement projected upward from the December low coincided with a second objective. Measured objectives are more reliable when two or more techniques forecast the same target area.

Several examples of upside and downside projections based on the Rule of Seven are shown in fig. 44 (May 1976 Copper). Note that the August peak of 66.60¢ was about 40 points *short* of the No. 2 objective, and about 40 points *above* the corresponding counter-swing objective shown in fig. 42. This "cluster" of two objectives arrived at by different techniques gave the correct area of the top by a very close margin. Similarly, the December low of 54.30¢ was predicted by the combination of a No. 2 downside objective and the swing measurement shown in fig. 41. In fig. 44 note also the year-end head-and-shoulders bottom that projected an upside objective at about the same level as the No. 2 upside objective by the Rule of Seven.

In fig. 45 (May 1976 Plywood) the minor upside objective No. 3

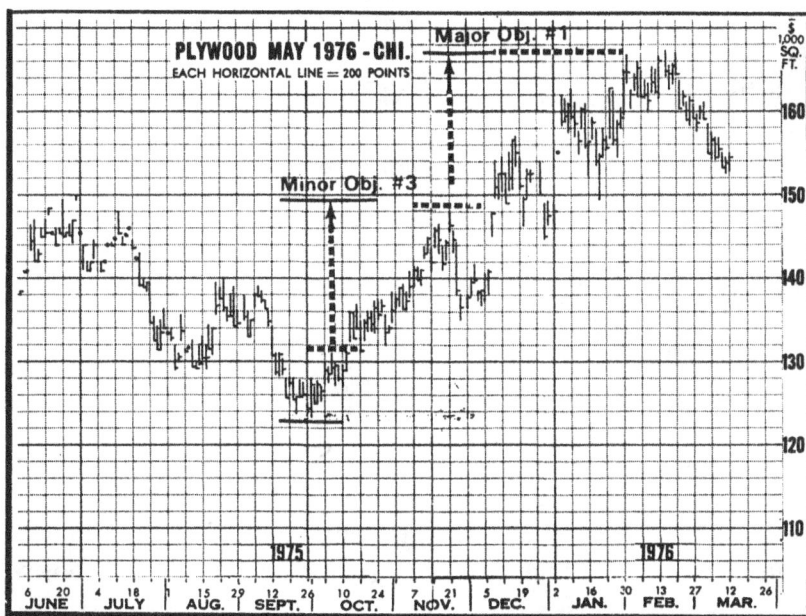

Figure 45. Rule of Seven—Minor and Major Objectives: As a general rule, the greater the magnitude and duration of the initial price swing, the greater the likelihood that the next swing will stop at the first objective. Initial price swings of small magnitude and short duration call for a subsequent move that is likely to skip the first and second minor objective and stop at the third or fourth minor objective. The first major objective was predicated on the larger October-November price swing.

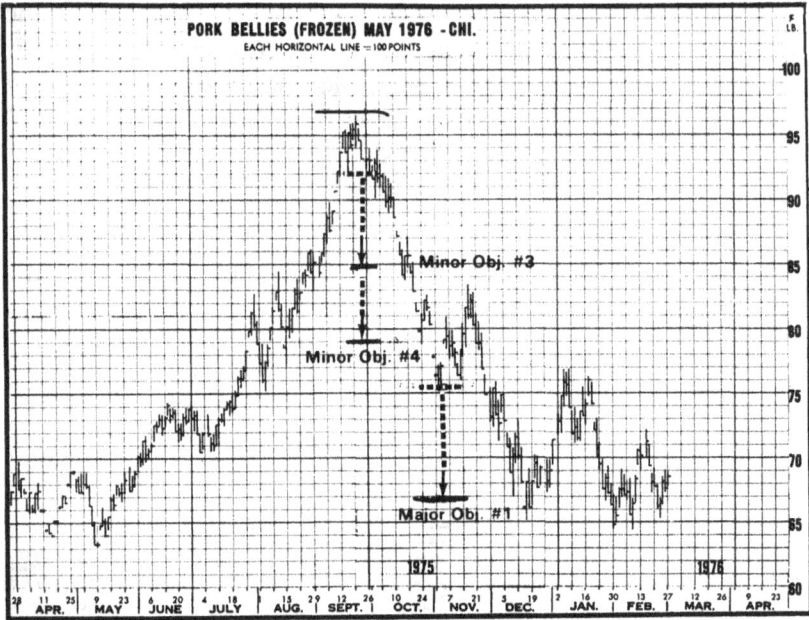

Figure 46. Rule of Seven Measurements: The initial brief four-day dip from the September peak called for a third or fourth minor downside objective. The big October downswing was used to project a first major objective.

by the Rule of Seven confirmed the counter-swing objective shown in fig. 43, from which level a sharp break in the market occurred. The later resumption of the uptrend in December permitted the projection of an almost perfect major No. 1 objective by the Rule of Seven.

In fig. 46 (May 1976 Pork Bellies) the initial major downswing went from the September high of 96.50¢ to the November low of 75.27¢. The difference, 2123 points, when multiplied by 1.40 and subtracted from the high of 96.50¢ gave an initial downside objective of 66.78¢, which was very close to the actual December low. Applying the Rule of Seven to the *minor trend*, the first minor downswing from the high of 96.50¢ took four days to bottom out at 91.52¢. This gave a No. 3 downside projection to 84.90¢ (reached in the third week of October) and also a No. 4 downside objective of 79.07¢, satisfied at the low of October 24.

The 17–35 Measurement

It is difficult to find a logical reason why many sustained commodity futures price moves congest or reverse after covering a distance equal to 17½% or 35% of the recent high or low price. Yet this happens so frequently that it must be more than just a coincidence. I suspect that those percentage moves may have a relationship to the constant-width curved channels described in Chapter 4. Since major-trend curved channels tend to have a vertical width that is roughly 10% of the price level, and the next larger channel has a width of about 20% of the price level, the 10% channel, moving up, might meet the descending 20% channel at about 17½% from the low. A 20% channel, by the same reasoning, might be stalled around 35%.

Whether this reasoning is logical or not, price objectives can often be accurately projected upside at 17½% and 35% of the price at the low, and the same percentages downside from a price peak. By the same reasoning, one would expect the minor 5% channel to meet opposition on a swing of perhaps 7½%. Although the minor swings can often be distorted by the effects of random walk, an inspection of price charts will indeed show that many short swings and reactions do conform to a 7½% measurement. At the other end of the spectrum, another 17½% can occasionally be added to the 35% measurement, to project a 52½% objective on more extensive moves.

A few examples of the 17-35 measurement are illustrated here. In fig. 47 (May 1976 Copper), the June low of 56.50¢ yields a 17½% upside objective of 66.40¢. The actual peak was 66.60¢, which in turn gave a 17½% downside objective of 54.95¢ compared with an actual low of 54.20¢. That low projected a 17½% upside objective of about 63.70¢, which was not very far from the temporary peak at 64.60¢.

In fig. 48 (May 1976 Lumber), the October low of $131.50 projected a 17½% upside objective of $154.50, which gave some temporary trouble to the advance; but the 35% upside objective of $177.50 was a close match to the important February high of $178.00. An interim 17½% measurement from the December low of $148.40 projected a high of $174.40, which closely matched the January peak.

In fig. 49 (April 1976 COMEX Gold), from the February 1975 peak around $207 the 17½ % and 35% downside projections gave objectives of $170.80 and $134.55, closely in line with the important lows of April and September.

Fig. 50 (May 1976 Plywood): From the contract low of $123.50, a 17½ % and 35% upside projection called for a move to $145.11 and $166.72, both of which proved to be quite accurate. Note the other confirming objectives in figs. 43 and 45 that supported the 17–35 measurements.

Fig. 51 (May 1976 N.Y. Silver): The April 1975 low was 435.80, giving a 17½ % upside objective of 512.06 (near the May high) and a 35% upside objective of 588.33, which was not quite reached. The peak was 567.50, from which level a 17½ % downside measurement gave a target of 468.19 (very near the September low) and a 35% target a bit too far at 368.88.

Fig. 52 (May 1976 Soybeans): The June 1975 low of 498 gave upside projections of 17½ % and 35% to 585 and 672, essentially in line with the important peaks of July and August. The August high of 680 projected a downside target of 561 (very close to the actual September low of 570), and the next target at 442 (compared with an actual low of 457½).

Fig. 53 (May 1976 Coffee "C"): The dynamic advance from the July low around 55¢ did not stop until it had satisfied the big 52½ % upside objective of 83.90¢. Following the prolonged correction to the November low of 75.50¢, the 17½ % and 35% measurements projected upside targets of 88.70¢ and 101.90¢.

Let's leave the price charts themselves for a while now, and talk about some simple mathematical indicators that can help you determine when a price trend is gaining or losing momentum.

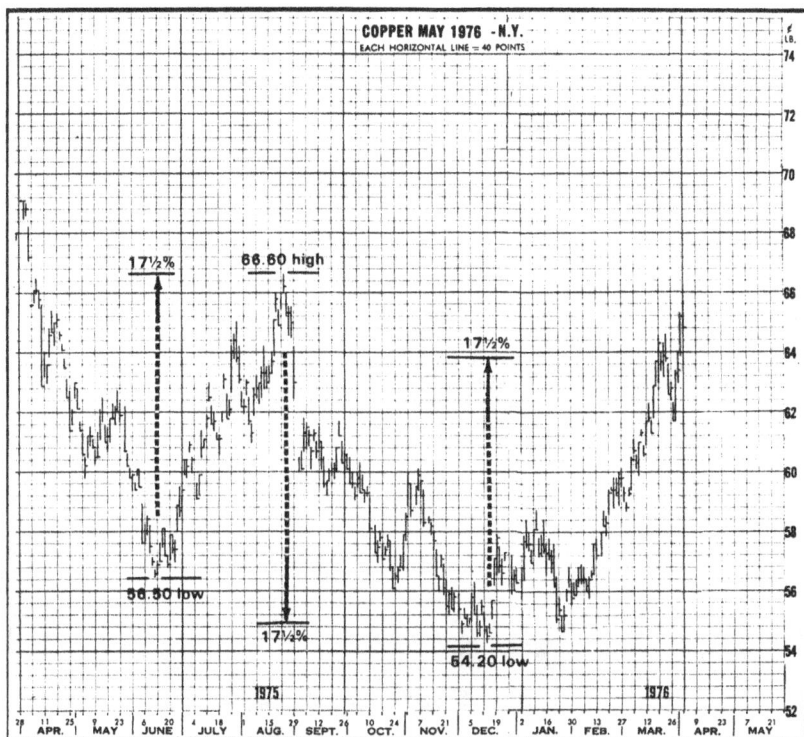

Figure 47. The 17–35 Measurement: Whatever the reason might be, many sustained price moves cover a distance equal to 17½% or 35% of the price at the starting point. In this example, the 17½% measurement was satisfied three times within a relatively short period of time.

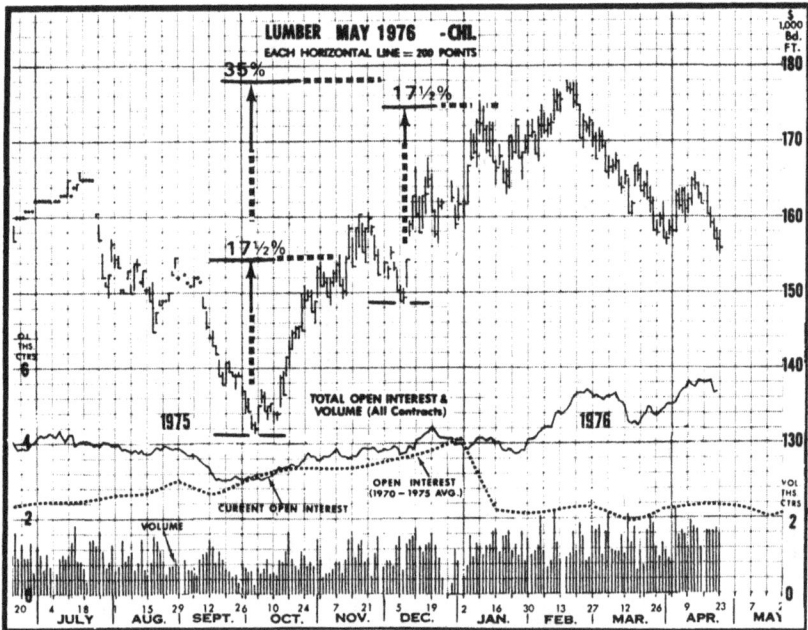

Figure 48. The 17–35 Measurement: On this chart, both the 17½% and 35% measurement proved meaningful.

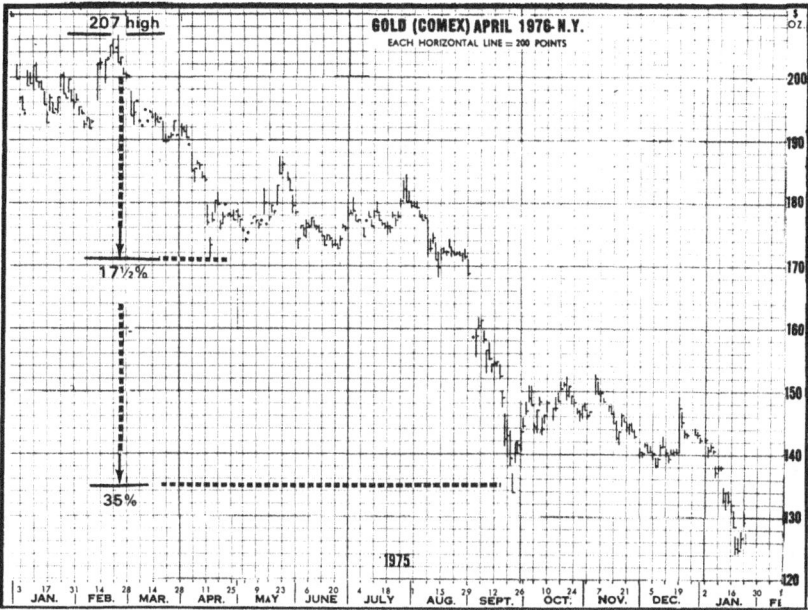

Figure 49. The 17–35 Measurement: The decline from the February peak stopped almost precisely at both the 17½% and the 35% objectives.

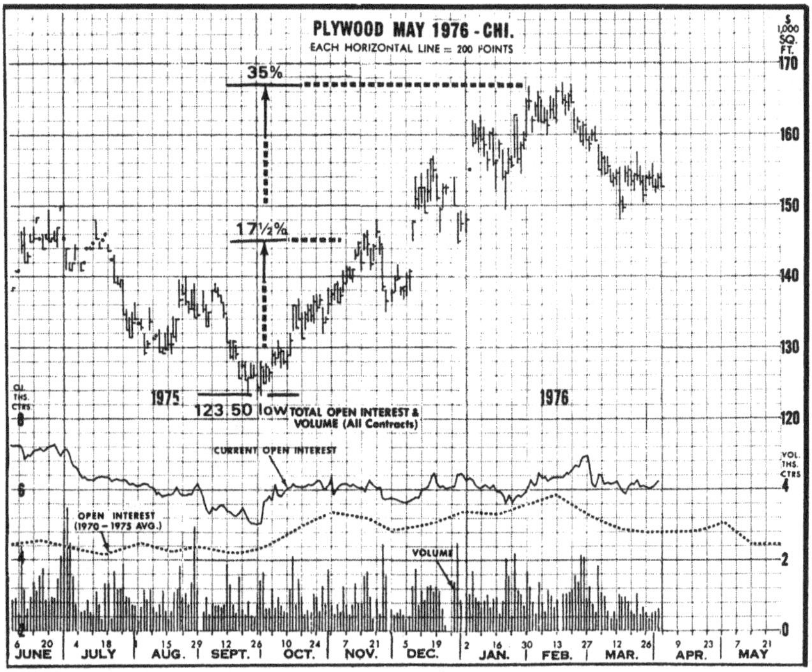

Figure 50. The 17–35 Measurement: The rally from the contract low made a minor top near the 17½% objective and a major top at the 35% target. Note that the 17½% measurement coincided with the Counter-Swing measurement shown in Figure 43.

Figure 51. The 17–35 Measurement: In this example, the 17½% targets were well satisfied but the 35% objectives were not quite reached.

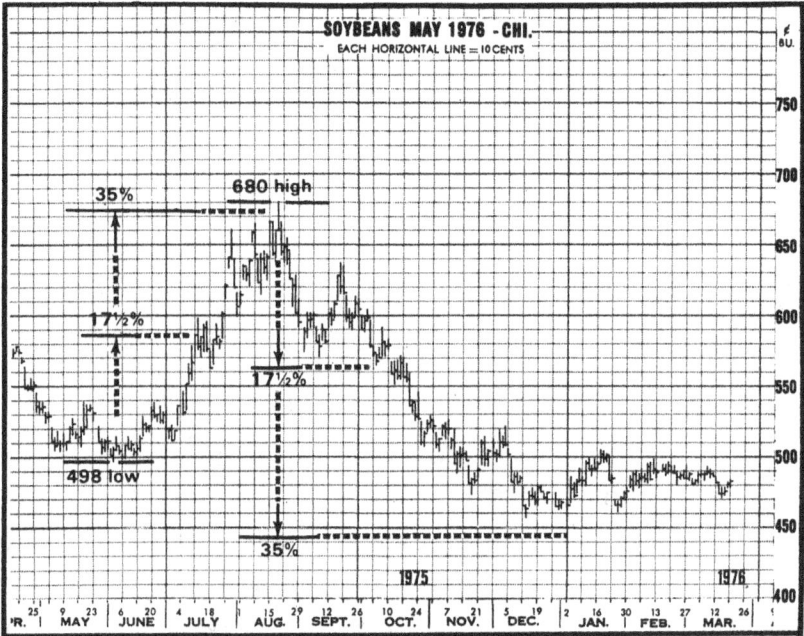

Figure 52. The 17–35 Measurement: Price movements in this market responded well to the 17½% and 35% measurements.

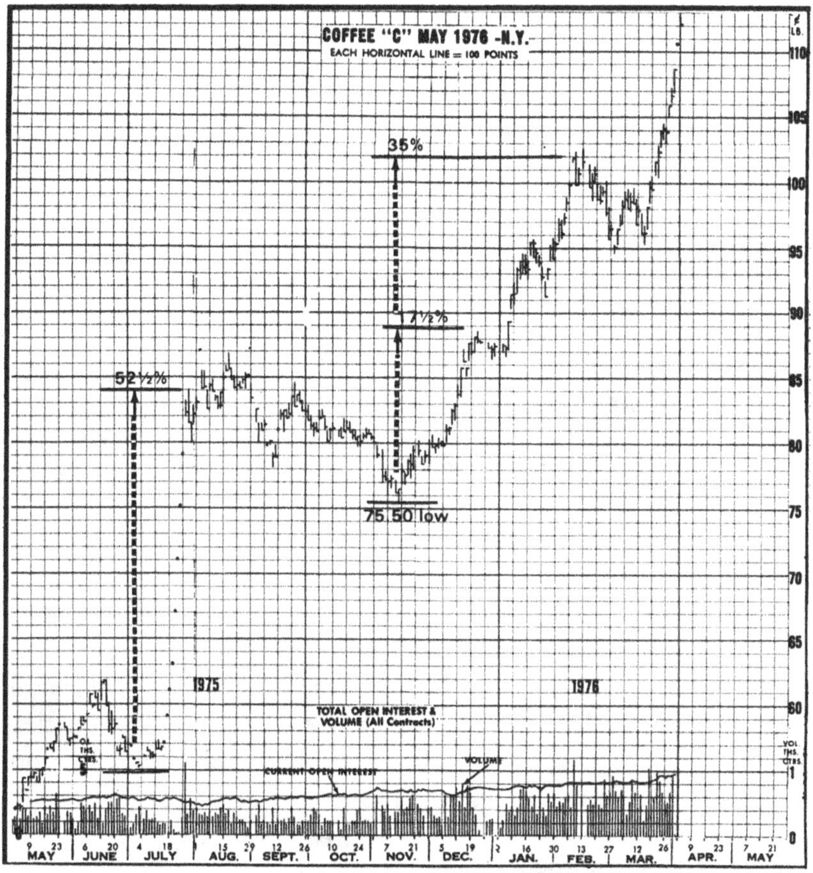

Figure 53. The 17–35 Measurement: The dynamic advance in July carried the market to the 52½% target area (the third 17–35 objective) before reacting. On the next upswing, resistance was encountered at the 17½% and 35% levels.

CHAPTER 6

Oscillator Techniques

The Function of Oscillators

Oscillators are tantalizing tools. They contain much information about the trend, but keep it all buried in such a confusing array of connected points that they almost seem intent on hiding their secrets from the chartist.

Oscillators tend to move in fairly well-defined trend patterns that often reverse direction in advance of the price trend itself. It is this characteristic that makes the oscillator valuable as a forecasting tool. Using hindsight, it is often relatively easy to see where the oscillator gave a clear warning of an impending reversal of trend. The problem is to convert those advance warnings into precise and profitable trading signals beforehand.

Technicians use oscillators in a variety of ways. When a market becomes "overbought" or "oversold," that condition is often revealed by an oscillator when it returns toward the zero line after previously moving to an extreme plus or minus level. Some chartists make use of relatively long-term oscillators as a guide to the reversal of the major or long-term trend. On this type of oscillator, a long-term trendline is usually drawn across the swings of the oscillator in the direction of the price trend. A penetration of that trendline by the oscillator signals the probable reversal of the trend. Other technicians make use of relatively short-term oscillators that can give well-defined signals of minor-trend reversals.

Relationship of Oscillators to Moving Averages

Net-change oscillators are indicators of the *velocity* of the price change, and in this respect they are closely related to moving averages. For example, let's compare a five-day Net-Change Oscillator with a five-day Moving Average, both based on daily closing prices. A five-day Net-Change Oscillator is constructed by plotting the plus or minus difference between the latest closing price and the closing price of five days ago. The plus or minus values are plotted each day above or below a zero line with a dot, and each day's dot is connected to the previous day's dot with a straight line. A five-day Moving Average is calculated by adding the closing prices of the last five days and dividing the sum by five. Each day a new closing price must be added to the old five-day total and the closing price of five days ago must be subtracted before dividing the new sum by five. The speed at which the five-day Moving Average advances or declines will depend on the difference between the latest closing price and the closing price of five days ago (which is to be dropped). *This difference is exactly what is plotted on the five-day Net-Change Oscillator.*

When any Net-Change Oscillator crosses from the plus to the minus side of the zero line, it means that the corresponding Moving Average has reversed direction from up to down. Conversely, when a Net-Change Oscillator crosses from minus to plus, the corresponding Moving Average is reversing from down to up. When a Net-Change Oscillator moves progressively higher on the plus side of the zero line, it indicates that the Moving Average is accelerating its advance. When the plus signs on the Net-Change Oscillator get smaller, the advance of the Moving Average is slowing down. On the minus side of the Net-Change Oscillator, the moving line tells in the same way whether the *decline* is accelerating or slowing down.

The relative importance of all changes in the movement of the corresponding Moving Average are reflected clearly in the Net-

Change Oscillator. Oscillators, therefore, extract much vital information about the character of the trend.

Variations in Oscillator Techniques

Oscillators are usually plotted on the basis of closing prices, but there are other techniques which can prove useful. For example, instead of plotting today's close versus some previous close, one can make a two-part oscillator (upper and lower) by plotting today's high versus some previous high on the upper section, and today's low versus some previous low on the lower section. The upper section would be used to detect the end of a downtrend; the lower section would be for following an uptrend. A similar type of double oscillator measures the swing of the market over a given period of time by plotting today's high versus some previous low (a fixed number of days back), and today's low versus the previous high the same number of days back. Changes in the direction of the price trend will often be signaled on such an oscillator before the price action itself gives a clear signal.

Another revealing oscillator is one that shows the difference between today's closing price and yesterday's *Moving Average*. If a five-day Moving Average is used for this purpose, the oscillator can be used for signaling a reversal of the minor trend. If longer-term Moving Averages are used, they will tend to identify changes in long-term trends. This type of oscillator would be utilized and interpreted in much the same way as the Daily-Net-Change Oscillator to be described next. Most oscillators will be found to be helpful indicators, some to a greater or lesser degree than others. After years of patiently testing different types of minor trend oscillators, I have come to favor the simplest of all oscillators—the Daily-Net-Change Oscillator of closing prices.

The Daily-Net-Change Oscillator

The Daily-Net-Change Oscillator of closing prices ("Daily NCO") is essentially a short-term indicator that identifies minor-trend reversals. It can be used alone or in conjunction with a longer term indicator as the basis for an Automatic Trading Method, subject to the limitations of the Principle of Selective Techniques described in the first chapter.

Stated briefly, the function of the Daily NCO is to warn of an impending change in the minor trend, and to instruct the chartist when and where to draw a valid trendline across the price action itself. A trendline signaled by the Daily NCO will sometimes coincide with the conventional trendline that might have been drawn anyway. However, in many instances the Daily NCO will help to avoid drawing a premature trendline, or it may indicate that the valid trendline is to be drawn along a steep and rapid move where one might normally hesitate to apply a trendline.

Since the value of the Daily NCO lies in its tendency to reverse its trend in advance of a reversal in the price trend itself, the question naturally arises as to what precise technique should be used to pinpoint the timing of the impending price trend reversal. The use of a trendline across the price action in conjunction with a warning signal on the Daily NCO was decided upon only after other alternatives were exhaustively tested and found to be less reliable. The warning signal, in most cases, meant that there was likely to be only one more brief surge in the direction of the trend before it reversed. But the warning was sometimes followed by only a one- or two-day pause and a resumption of the prevailing trend, followed later by a new warning signal. The application of a trendline across the price action, subject to certain precise rules of treatment, was found to avoid many premature signals and generally to signal a valid reversal.

Construction of the Daily-Net-Change Oscillator

Oscillators are most helpful and easiest to use when they are plotted on the same chart as the price action, along the same time scale. The Daily NCO is best plotted in open space near the top or bottom of the price chart.

A horizontal line should first be drawn across the chart to represent the zero value. The value scale, plus and minus, should generally be based on the same scale that is used for plotting the prices, with room above and below the zero line to allow for extensive movement.

Each day after the close of the market the daily net change (today's settling price versus yesterday's settling price) is plotted as a plus or minus value by placing a dot at the proper point above or below the zero line. For example, if the market closes with a gain of, say, 50 points over the previous close, a dot is placed on the oscillator at 50 points above the zero line on the vertical line that corresponds to that day. As each day's net change is plotted on the oscillator, the two latest points are connected with a straight line. The resulting picture will be a series of irregular zigzag swings above and below the zero line.

Forecasting Minor Trend Reversals
With the Daily-Net-Change Oscillator

Although the zigzag swings of the Daily NCO move horizontally along the zero line, there are brief up and down trends *on the oscillator* along the way; these are characterized by a series of higher tops and higher bottoms, or lower tops and lower bottoms. These oscillator trends will not always coincide timewise with similar trends in the price movement. When prices are making a low, for example, the oscillator may already be in an uptrend. What we want to accomplish first is to draw a valid trendline *on the oscillator.* However, that trendline on the oscillator must not be drawn until the price trend itself is moving in the same direction as the oscillator trend, as indicated by a previous signal given by the oscillator.

Therefore, the first rule to observe is: To be valid, a trendline on the oscillator must coincide with the present trend in the price action itself.

Once the appropriate oscillator trendline has been drawn across two or more points on the oscillator, the penetration of the trendline on the oscillator serves as a "warning" that a reversal of price trend may be near. This "warning" penetration on the oscillator tells you to get ready to draw a trendline across the price action itself. (Note that although the trendlines on the oscillator are based on

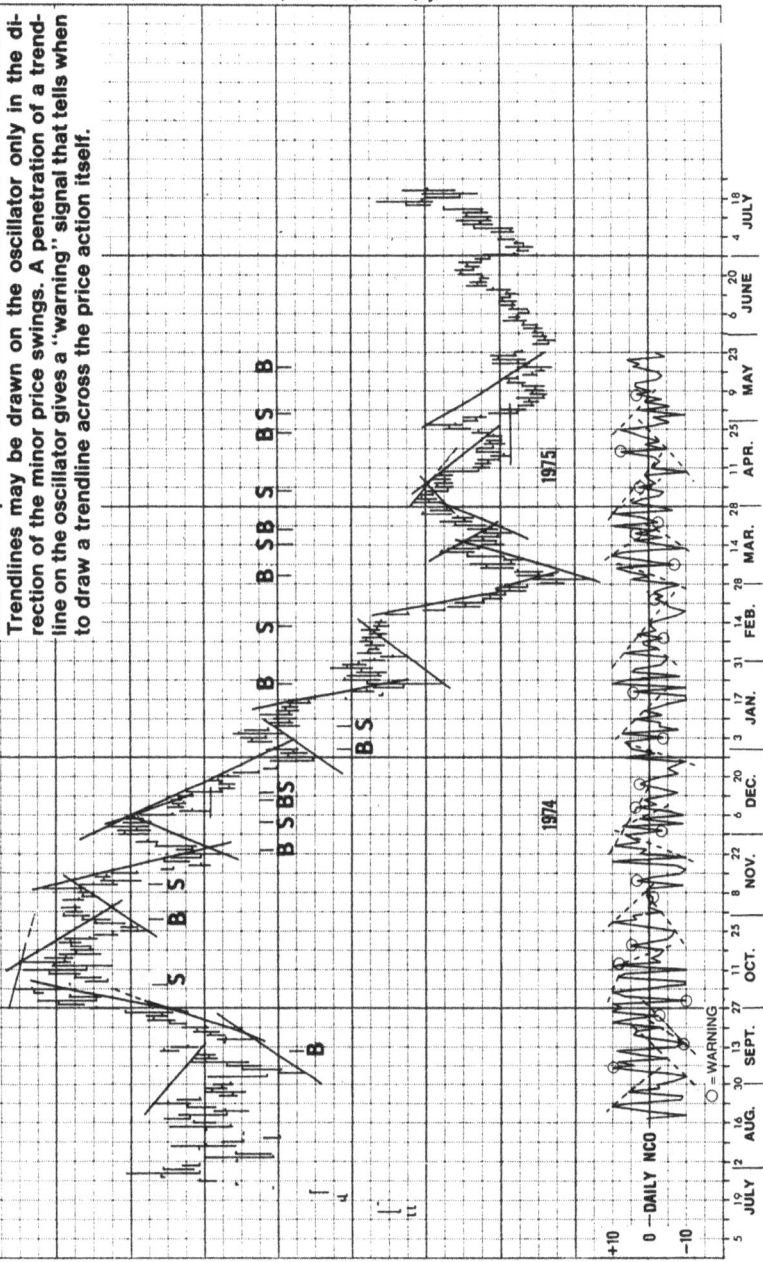

Figure 54. Daily Net Change Oscillator: The difference between each day's closing price and the previous close is plotted as a plus or minus value along a zero line, and the successive points are connected to form the oscillator. Trendlines may be drawn on the oscillator only in the direction of the minor price swings. A penetration of a trendline on the oscillator gives a "warning" signal that tells when to draw a trendline across the price action itself.

101

closing prices, the trendlines across the price action will use the daily high-low ranges.)

When the "warning" penetration appears on the oscillator, there are two important conditions that must be met before the trendline can be drawn on the price chart: (1) The oscillator "warning" must first be "completed" by a one-day return move *toward* the zero line on the oscillator; and, (2) the price movement itself must also "complete" its reaction by resuming its trend for one day. The price reaction will be considered "completed" when the daily high-low range resumes the trend by moving in the direction of the prevailing trend for at least one day, and when the closing price also resumes the trend by showing a close with a net change in the direction of the trend.

Thus, the second rule to be observed is: A trendline on the price chart cannot be drawn until the warning signal of the oscillator is "completed," both on the oscillator and on the price chart itself.

Experience with the Daily NCO has shown that some trendlines on the price chart will hug the day-to-day price movement so closely that a slight slowing down in the progress of the trend could give a false penetration. The remedy is to require both a penetration of the previous day's range and a penetration of the trendline. This requirement gives rise to the third rule:

When a trendline has been drawn across the price movement in accordance with a signal of the Daily NCO, the penetration of that trendline is valid only if and when the previous day's range is also penetrated in that same direction.

It should also be noted that if the critical level of that previous day's range lines up closely with the level of the previous two or three days, then a penetration of the extreme price of that small sideways pattern is needed to make the penetration of the trendline valid.

After a reversal of trend has been signaled, the new trend will be without a protective trendline until a new trendline can be drawn on the oscillator and a warning has been completed. In the interim, the outermost swing of the previous trend must be used temporarily as the valid penetration point for a reversal of the price trend. For example, if a valid downtrend line has been penetrated on the upside (giving a "buy" signal), the new temporary "sell" signal will be a downside penetration of the low of the downtrend just ended until a new uptrend can be drawn in accordance with a signal of the oscillator. If such a temporary signal is activated, it means that the previous penetration of the trendline was "false." This leads to the final rule of the Daily NCO:

If a whipsaw occurs as a result of a reversal of trend signaled before a trendline across the new price action can be drawn in accordance with the rules, then the previous trendline that was falsely penetrated must be redrawn to fit the revised trend.

The one exception to the above rule would be in the event that a flag-like reaction takes shape in a direction opposite to the main trend. If no oscillator warning occurs promptly, see if it is possible to apply a "Reaction Predicted Trendline" as described in Chapter 3. A whipsaw loss that would otherwise have been taken might thus be avoided with the use of that supplementary technique.

It should be noted that not every trendline on the price chart (drawn as a result of a warning signal on the oscillator) results in a penetration and trend reversal. The price trend may accelerate at a steeper angle, leaving the trendline intact. In such cases, the oscillator will usually form a new series of zigzag swings in the direction of the price trend, permitting a new warning signal to be given and calling for a new and steeper trendline to be drawn across the price movement.

The application of the Daily NCO in accordance with the above four rules is shown in the chart of July 1975 Corn, fig. 54. Many of the reversal signals occurred within a day or two of a top or bottom. A few signals proved false. I believe the example shown can be considered as fairly typical of the average results.

Minor Trend Signals on a Five-Day Net-Change Oscillator

Another oscillator technique that can signal minor trend reversals makes use of a 5-day Net-Change Oscillator (NCO) of closing prices. While the 5-day NCO at first sight does not appear to be as sensitive as the Daily NCO, it can be made to give approximately the same signals in a different way. One shortcoming, however, is that the signals on the 5-day NCO will always be given on the close rather than during the trading session. The 5-day NCO is constructed by plotting the net change between the latest closing price and the closing price five days ago. When no holidays intervene, the comparison will be Monday's close versus the previous Monday, Tuesday versus the previous Tuesday, and so forth. If a holiday intervenes, a day is skipped; e.g., Tuesday will be versus the previous Monday.

It will probably be found most convenient to plot the 5-day NCO at half the scale of the price chart; for example, if each horizontal line of the price chart represents a 10-point change in price, each line on the oscillator should represent a 20-point change.

As in the case of the Daily NCO, the 5-day NCO makes use of trendlines across the oscillator. For catching the minor trend, an effective type of trendline for the 5-day NCO is one that is somewhat similar in principle to the "Final Predicted Trendline" described in Chapter 3, as follows: If the 5-day NCO is zigzagging upward, a "channel guideline" must first be drawn across two successive tops on the oscillator, and then a parallel uptrend line must be projected from the outermost intra-day dip of that uptrend. *The downside penetration of that parallel uptrend line on the oscillator is a signal to sell.* Similarly, when the 5-day NCO is zigzagging downward, a "channel guideline" is drawn across two successive dips on the oscillator, and a parallel downtrend line is projected from the outermost intra-day rally on the oscillator. The upside penetration of that downtrend line on the oscillator is a "buy" signal. Note that no trendlines are drawn on the price action itself; the 5-day NCO gives its signal independently. Fig. 55 demonstrates the use of the 5-day NCO on the July 1975 Corn contract.

Longer-Term Use of the Five-Day Net-Change Oscillator

The 5-day NCO has another interesting characteristic that can often be put to profitable use in longer-term trends. During a down-

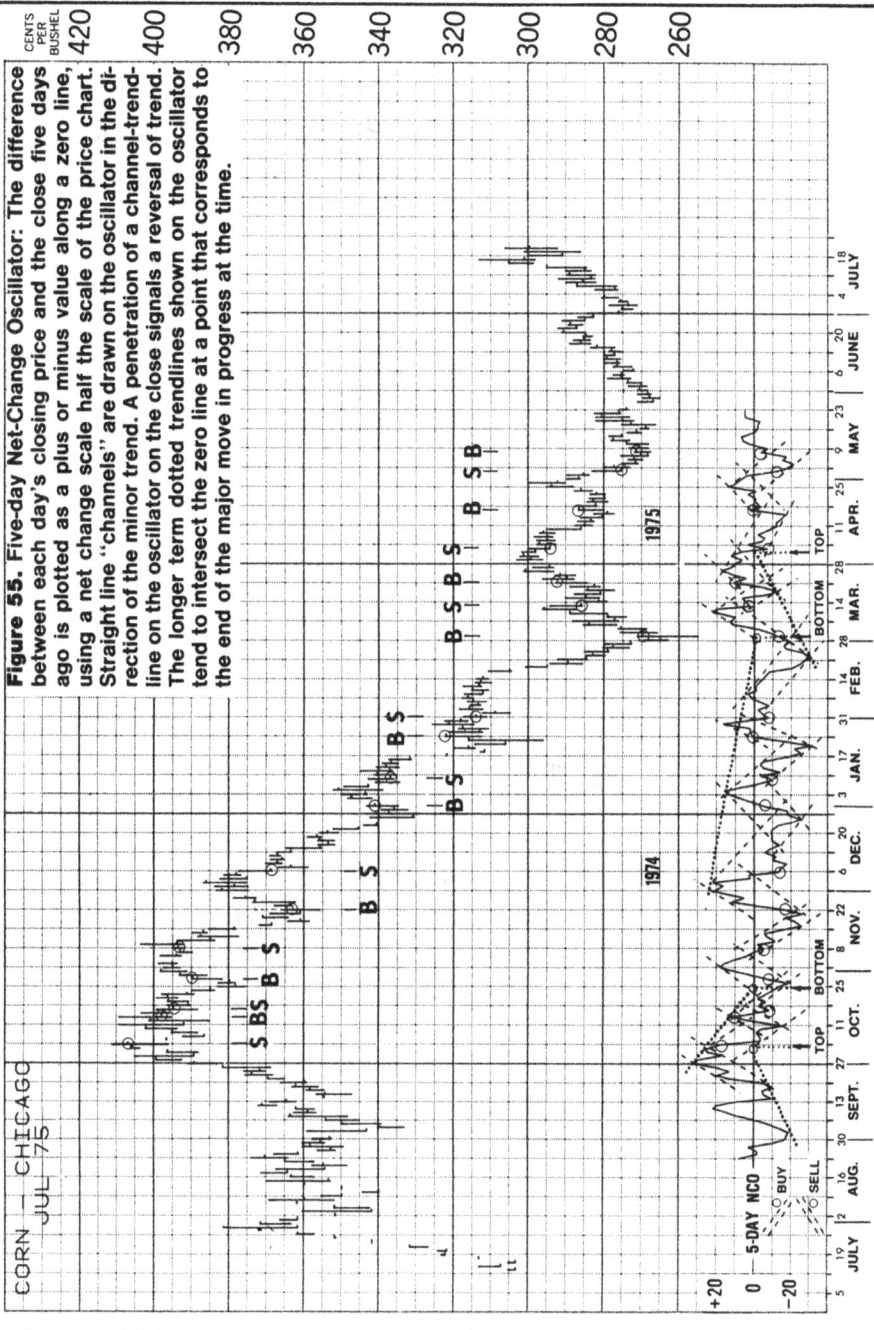

Figure 55. Five-day Net-Change Oscillator: The difference between each day's closing price and the close five days ago is plotted as a plus or minus value along a zero line, using a net change scale half the scale of the price chart. Straight line "channels" are drawn on the oscillator in the direction of the minor trend. A penetration of a channel-trendline on the oscillator in the direction of the minor trend. A penetration of a channel-trendline on the oscillator signals a reversal of trend. The longer term dotted trendlines shown on the oscillator tend to intersect the zero line at a point that corresponds to the end of the major move in progress at the time.

trend there is a tendency for the PLUS oscillations to get smaller as the decline progresses, and during an uptrend the MINUS oscillations tend to get smaller. *A trendline drawn across those diminishing oscillations on a 5-day NCO in the direction of the price trend will often intersect the zero line at a point that corresponds to the time the move will be completed.*

Although its predictions are often uncannily accurate, this last function of the 5-day NCO sometimes misfires and must therefore be used with caution and in conjunction with other technical indicators. It is more dependable in timing the *end* of an upward or downward phase of the market than in timing a *reversal* of trend. It is best used as a guide for taking profits rather than for establishing a new position in the opposite direction.

In Fig. 55, the dotted trendlines on the 5-day NCO illustrate this technique. Note that the October 4 peak corresponds to the intersection of an uptrend line with the zero line of the oscillator. The short-term dip that bottomed on October 25 was also pinpointed by the intersection of a downtrend line on the oscillator. The timing of the major V-bottom that occurred in the first week of March was predicted by a long-term downtrend line across the November-January peaks of the oscillator. And the short-term top the first week of April was accurately forecast by the intersection of an uptrend line across the February-March lows of the oscillator.

We mentioned moving averages briefly earlier in this chapter. Now let's take a closer look at what they are and how they work.

CHAPTER 7

Use of Moving Averages in Trend Trading Methods

Catching That Big Move

I have often thought that the best way to trade the commodity markets would be to just sit back and wait for a major signal to get aboard that big move when it comes. And sometimes you do get a clear indication from the fundamentals and a clear major signal on the charts. Some of those convincing signals *are* followed by an extensive and sustained price move, but so many other times the market just jiggles around for weeks or months before it starts to move, or fizzles out and doesn't get going at all. And how about the many times the market just takes off without any obvious warning? It would certainly be ideal if we could just wait for those golden opportunities, and trade only when we know a big move is coming!

If you base your trading method on such a plan you may be

* With apologies to Alfred, Lord Tennyson's "Charge of the Light Brigade."

doomed to disappointment. This does not mean that you cannot catch those big moves. You can catch *every one of them* in every market you trade. But to do so, you must follow a trend trading plan. That means you must be in those markets trading the lesser moves, and taking the whipsaw losses, while you keep probing for those bigger moves.

Advantages and Shortcomings of Moving Averages

For the chartist who decides to follow an *automatic trend trading plan* for his buy and sell signals, moving averages provide an effective means for doing so. However, it will be recalled that in Chapter 1 reference was made to a so-called Principle of Selective Techniques. It was noted that automatic trend methods that work well in one commodity market will not necessarily work well in other commodities. Wheat, Pork Bellies, Plywood, Silver and T-Bills, for example, are vastly different commodities. One should not be surprised if the day-to-day price movements in each of those markets fail to respond equally well to the same trend-following techniques.

Nevertheless, moving averages enable a trader to put into practice the ideal plan of cutting losses short and letting profits ride.

There are countless variations in the way moving averages can be computed and applied. However, no matter what procedure one adopts, the same basic advantages and disadvantages will undoubtedly be evident in the course of trading.

The basic advantages of a moving average trend system are:

1. Risks are automatically limited and losses can usually be minimized.
2. Positions are established automatically in the right direction at the onset of a sustained move, and this tends to maximize profits.

The basic disadvantages are:

1. During trendless periods and periods of erratic price movement, repeated whipsaw losses may be taken, and the whipsaws

cannot be avoided without abandoning the trading method altogether.

2. Although net gains are likely to result in the long run, the actual number of losing trades is likely to exceed the number of profitable trades, perhaps by a wide margin.

It takes considerable self-discipline to stay with a trading plan when losses occur in rapid succession, but the payoff comes when a market begins to move in a well-defined trend and your trading system has automatically put you on the right side of a sustained price move. The frustration of having been whipsawed is then offset by the elation of successfully riding a trend.

Trend-following methods are not easy to live with. No matter what rules of procedure you follow, there will be occasions when you find yourself selling at the bottom of a dip or buying at the top of a rally, and wondering if you should stay with such a system. If you then alter your method or your rules in order to avoid such a situation in the future, you will probably find that you are simply exchanging one bad feature for another. The reason for this is simply that price trends are rarely orderly and regular. There is a considerable amount of random price change taking place at all times within the trend, and those random, erratic price movements are the cause of most whipsaw losses. Unfortunately, the timing and magnitude of such random price swings are, by their very nature, largely unpredictable, and the resulting whipsaws cannot be completely avoided in any type of trend-following plan.

It is not the purpose of this chapter to recommend any specific trend trading methods or computer-type systems, but merely to discuss the use of Moving Averages as trading tools, and to describe some variations in the way they can be used.

Any carefully planned trend-following method, no matter how devised, will almost certainly catch a portion of the profit in any sustained price move; and, will just as certainly be whipsawed during relatively trendless periods. It is difficult to predict with certainty that any one particular trend-following method will prove superior to all others, even if one goes by the track record. The past record, excellent as it may have been, cannot be a guarantee of future performance.

It is hoped, however, that the ideas presented here may prove useful as a foundation for traders to set up their own trend-following methods if they wish to do so.

Variations in the Use of Moving Averages

As already mentioned, there are countless ways in which moving averages can be computed and applied. Before setting up a moving average trading system, certain decisions must be made. For example:

•The daily price range consists of an opening, high, low and close. Which price or prices are to be used in the computation of the moving average?

•There are short-term and longer-term trends all in progress at the same time. Which trend is the one to be traded, and what period of time should the moving average cover?

•Should a single moving average be used, or some combination of moving averages? And if two or more are used, how should they be treated in relation to each other?

•If a trend reversal is to be signaled by a price penetration of the moving average, how much of a penetration should be considered valid? Should today's moving average be applied to tomorrow's action, or should the moving average be advanced one or more days?

•Should the moving average be a conventional arithmetical mean (the sum of the prices divided by the number of prices), or should it be a weighted average, a median average, a midpoint value, or some other type of average?

There are no pat answers to these questions. While different results will undoubtedly be obtained by different methods, all moving average methods are tied to a trend, and in the long run almost any variation will be found to have merit, especially when applied selectively to markets that have a history of responding well to that method. The choice of the method or methods to be used by a trader, then, is largely a matter of personal preference.

Types of Moving Averages

The most frequently used moving average is the "simple" moving average obtained by adding the closing prices for a certain number of days and then dividing the sum by the number of days. However, some traders prefer more complex types of averages which incorporate various weighting factors in their calculations.

For example, a simple 10-day moving average attaches the same weight to the closing price 10 days ago as it does to yesterday's close. Many analysts feel that more recent price action deserves greater importance, which led to the development of the "linearly weighted" moving average. In a 10-day linearly weighted average, yesterday's close would be multiplied by 10, the previous day's close by nine, and so forth. The sum would then be divided by the total of the digits 1, 2, . . . , 10 (=55) to get the required average.

This type of average attaches greater weight to the most recent price action, but is still open to criticism for completely ignoring the trading that took place prior to the first day included in the calculations. The "exponentially smoothed" moving average corrects this possible deficiency by incorporating a potentially infinite time span. An exponentially smoothed average attaches the greatest weight to the most recent price and a gradually decreasing weight to each preceding price back to the onset of trading. The exact formula for calculating the exponentially smoothed weights is somewhat complex, and the calculations themselves require the aid of a computer. For this reason, exponentially smoothed averages are impractical for most traders to construct themselves.

Despite their greater sophistication and complexity, it is questionable whether the various types of weighted moving averages perform significantly better than the simple averages. Some recent research reported later in this chapter suggests that the simple averages actually outperform their more complicated counterparts, and that all have their share of false signals and whipsaws.

What Length Should the Moving Average Be?

Should one use a 3-day moving average, a 5-day, 10-day, 20-day or what? One of the advantages of moving averages is that it is possible, with the help of a computer, to approach this question systematically and objectively. A pennant or a downward sloping wedge is always, to some extent, in the eye of the beholder, but a penetration of a moving average line is precise and unequivocal. Given a good data base and enough computer time, it is possible to experiment with an endless variety of moving averages and see how each would have performed in the past.

Comprehensive work along these lines has been done by Frank Hochheimer, who published his results in the 1978 Commodity Year Book (published by: Commodity Research Bureau, Inc., 1 Liberty Plaza, New York, New York 10006). Mr. Hochheimer tested simple, exponentially smoothed, and linearly weighted moving averages ranging in length from 3 to 70 days on each contract of 13 different commodity futures traded between 1970 and 1976. To evaluate the performance of each average, he attached certain weights to each of a variety of features deemed desirable in a system's performance. Thus, total net profit was given considerable weight, but such items as the longest string of losing trades and the percentage of profitable trades were also taken into consideration. Hochheimer's results are summarized in the accompanying tables.

Note that the length of the "best" moving average varied considerably from commodity to commodity. For example, when a simple moving average was applied to soybeans, the best results were obtained from a length of 55 days. For pork bellies, the best length was only 19 days. This is consistent with the popular image of bellies as an especially volatile commodity with many price swings of short duration.

These simulated results also show a tremendous range of optimum profitabilities. Sugar and soybeans yielded huge net profits using each of the three different types of moving averages, but none of the averages tested was able to generate worthwhile gains from

Table 1
Theoretical Trading Results from Simple Moving Averages

	Best Average	Cumulative Profits or Losses (Net)	Largest String of Losses	Number Trades	Number Profitable Trades	Number Losing Trades	Ratio: #Profits #Trades
Cocoa	54	$ 87,957	$−14,155	600	157	443	.262
Corn	43	24,646	− 6,537	565	126	439	.223
Sugar	60	270,402	−15,563	492	99	393	.201
Cotton	57	68,685	−11,330	641	121	520	.189
Silver	19	42,920	−15,285	1,393	429	964	.308
Copper	59	165,143	− 7,687	432	158	274	.366
Soybeans	55	222,195	−10,800	728	151	577	.207
Soybean Meal	68	22,506	−20,900	704	148	556	.210
Wheat	41	65,806	−12,550	480	124	356	.258
Pork Bellies	19	97,925	− 9,498	774	281	493	.363
Soybean Oil	69	89,416	− 8,920	586	122	464	.208
Plywood	68	1,622	− 3,929	372	98	274	.263
Hogs	16	35,595	− 7,190	1,093	318	775	.291

Table 2
Theoretical Trading Results from Linearly Weighted Moving Averages

	Best Average	Cumulative Profits or Losses (Net)	Largest String of Losses	Number Trades	Number Profitable Trades	Number Losing Trades	Ratio: #Profits #Trades
Cocoa	52	$ 74,450	$− 8,773	796	206	590	.259
Corn	65	21,779	− 5,487	524	118	406	.225
Sugar	58	233,822	−14,063	707	149	558	.211
Cotton	69	44,395	−18,070	731	139	592	.190
Silver	45	− 34,435	−20,920	1,036	297	739	.287
Copper	68	124,848	−13,924	541	179	362	.331
Soybeans	42	178,261	−19,100	892	213	697	.239
Soybean Meal	41	31,385	−20,900	1,128	235	893	.208
Wheat	70	52,495	− 9,000	403	94	309	.233
Pork Bellies	28	81,625	− 9,222	815	267	548	.328
Soybean Oil	34	106,996	− 5,470	1,198	303	895	.253
Plywood	70	− 22,273	− 5,138	470	109	361	.232
Hogs	70	9,981	− 9,314	509	131	378	.257

plywood. This, too, is consistent with intuition, since soybeans and sugar had enormous bull and bear markets during the testing period, while plywood spent the majority of its time in relatively narrow trading ranges.

Naturally, there is no guarantee that what would have worked in 1970–76 will work as well in the future. Still, the results are instructive because they seem to confirm that moving average trading can be quite profitable. They also suggest that longer term averages perform better than shorter term averages when a single moving aver-

Table 3

Theoretical Trading Results from Exponentially Smoothed Moving Averages

	Best Average	Cumulative Profits or Losses (Net)	Largest String of Losses	Number Trades	Number Profitable Trades	Number Losing Trades	Ratio: #Profits #Trades
Cocoa	57	$ 99,080	$—10,363	619	166	453	.268
Corn	68	15,119	— 4,901	471	98	373	.208
Sugar	69	172,985	—15,921	591	105	486	.178
Cotton	70	35,855	—15,075	605	113	492	.187
Silver	60	— 61,400	—18,965	914	205	709	.224
Copper	68	136,130	— 5,886	450	150	300	.333
Soybeans	60	197,218	—13,600	708	142	566	.201
Soybean Meal	62	— 8,486	—18,200	840	162	678	.193
Wheat	70	13,570	—11,150	421	75	346	.178
Pork Bellies	12	80,303	—11,177	1,217	401	816	.329
Soybean Oil	66	82,904	— 6,730	677	160	517	.236
Plywood	69	— 24,526	— 5,002	467	104	363	.223
Hogs	67	— 11,834	—11,863	504	112	392	.222

Table 4

Most Consistent Indicators—Simple vs. Exponential vs. Linearly Weighted Moving Averages

Commodity	No. Days	Type of Average
Cocoa	57-day	Exponentially Smoothed
Corn	43-day	Simple
Sugar	60-day	Simple
Cotton	57-day	Simple
Silver	19-day	Simple
Copper	59-day	Simple
Soybeans	55-day	Simple
Soybean Meal	41-day	Linearly Weighted
Wheat	41-day	Simple
Pork Bellies	19-day	Simple
Soybean Oil	34-day	Linearly Weighted
Plywood	68-day	Simple
Hogs	16-day	Simple

age of closing prices is used. Of the 39 separate tests reported by Hochheimer, the shortest optimum average was 12 days, and only four optimum averages were shorter than 20 days. In contrast, 20 of the best performing averages were 60 days or longer.

Using Moving Averages in Combination with Each Other

Since moving averages tend to smooth out the irregularities of the trend, a pronounced change in the direction of a moving average generally corresponds to a change in direction of the price trend in that commodity. However, by the time the moving average turns, the price itself will usually be well on its way in the new direction. The tendency for this kind of signal to lag behind the market makes its use in that way open to question.

As an alternative to the above, one might follow a plan that utilizes a combination of three different moving averages. For the method to be described here, some researchers have found that 4-day, 9-day and 18-day moving averages comprise a useful combination for catching the major trend. These moving averages would be the conventional arithmetical means of daily closing prices. If the three moving averages are plotted simultaneously on a price chart, it will be seen that during a downtrend, for example, the 4-day moving average will lead the decline, followed by the 9-day and the 18-day. The 4-day moving average will follow the downward price movement closely, the 9-day will usually lag behind, and the 18-day will follow at a still higher level. There will be a tendency for the three moving averages to maintain those positions relative to each other as long as the trend is downward. Some intermingling might occur during pauses in the decline, but the moving averages are not likely to completely reverse their relative positions as long as the main trend continues to point downward.

Once the trend reverses to the upside, however, the 4-day moving average will move above both the 9-day and the 18-day, and the 9-day moving average will rise above the 18-day. As soon as all three become realigned in that bullish position, the upturn will have been established. This type of indicator is likely to give its signals relatively far from actual tops and bottoms since it is a major trend indicator, but its signal is likely to be more enduring than the signal of the single major trend moving average. As with all trend-following methods, this system will work best during extended price moves, and will have its share of whipsaws during prolonged periods of price stabilization.

There is another way of using moving averages in combination with each other that is more closely related to the short-term price action. A short-term moving average (based on the prevailing period of the minor trend cycle), and a long-term moving average (based on the next larger cycle) are plotted on the chart along with the daily price range. The general idea is that a price penetration of the short-term moving average signals a reversal of the minor trend, while a price penetration of both moving averages signals a major reversal of trend. Positions would be taken only in the direction of the major trend as determined by the latest penetration of the longer-term moving average. The short-term moving average would be used for liquidating positions and for reinstating them in the direction of the major trend. The position would therefore be neutral part of the time.

My preference is for *moving average channels;* that is, a twin set of moving averages, one of the daily highs and one of the daily lows, with all moving averages advanced a few days ahead of the market, as described in the next section.

Positioning the Moving Average in Relation to Price

If a simple moving average (arithmetical mean) of closing prices is plotted on a price chart at the vertical line corresponding to the day following the last day of the moving average series (a one-day advance), the closing price is likely to whipsaw the moving average frequently while on its way in the prevailing direction of the trend. By advancing the moving average farther ahead of that last price, the moving average is better able to function as a calculated trendline, occasionally stopping reactions, but usually remaining at a discreet distance from the swings of the closing price. If the moving average is properly advanced, it is more likely to give a valid signal of trend reversal when penetrated.

The same principle applies if one uses a moving average "channel" consisting of a moving average of the daily highs and one of the daily lows. In an uptrend, only the lower moving average is utilized; in a downtrend, the upper line is the one that is used, giving a reversal signal when penetrated by the price in the course of the day's trading. After numerous tests with different sized moving averages, I have found that there appears to be a correlation between the time period covered by the moving average and the number of days it should be advanced to be most effective.

I have come to the conclusion that the best fit of a short-term moving average requires the moving average to be advanced the number of days equal to the *square root of the time period of the moving average.* For example, since the square root of 9 is 3, a 9-day moving average channel should be advanced three days. This means, of course, that each day's price action must be judged in relation to the 9-day moving average calculated three days ago.

The scale works out about as follows:

Number of Days in Moving Average	Number of Trading Days to be Advanced
2 to 4 days	$\sqrt{4}$ = 2 days
5 to 9 days	$\sqrt{9}$ = 3 days
10 to 16 days	$\sqrt{16}$ = 4 days
17 to 25 days	$\sqrt{25}$ = 5 days

A 5-day moving average channel would therefore be plotted three days ahead. This means that if the 5-day period ends on a Friday, the moving average of that 5-day period would be applied to next Wednesday's trading session, Monday's moving average would apply to the following Thursday's market action, etc. Holidays should be treated the same as Saturdays and Sundays. Only trading days should be considered.

Using theoretical cycles, it is possible to demonstrate the theoretical correctness of using moving averages with a time period equal to a cyclical period, as well as the advisability of advancing the moving average a few days ahead in accordance with the square root rule described above.

This principle is demonstrated in fig. 56. The simulated daily closing prices are based on the sum of five different cycles plus a base price of 1000. Each cycle is three times longer and double the magnitude of the next smaller cycle. The smallest cycles are a 5-day cycle and a 15-day cycle. In theory, then, a 5-day moving average advanced three days, and a 15-day moving average advanced four days should effectively catch the main swings of those cycles. Both moving averages in their advanced position are shown in fig. 56, where their close adherence to their respective trends is quite obvious.

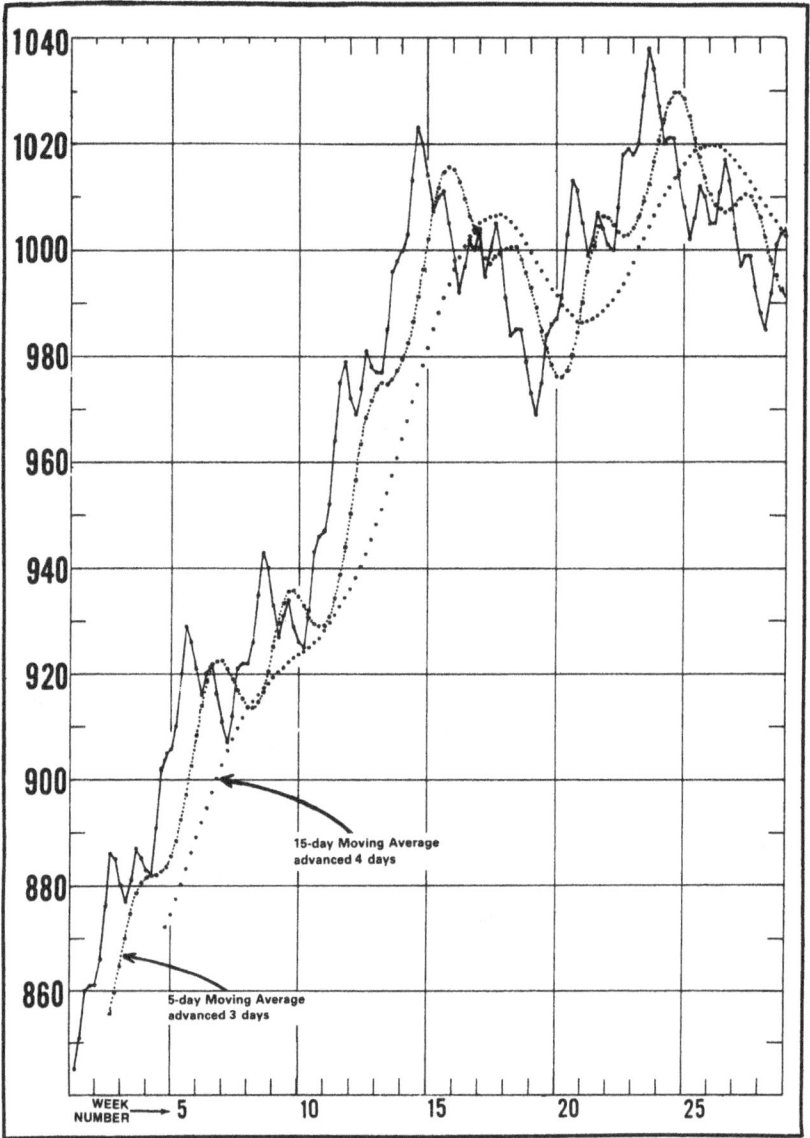

Figure 56. Five-day and 15-day Moving Averages Advanced According to
Square Root Rule in Theoretical Trend Containing 5-day and 15-day Cycles: The
simulated daily closing prices are based on the sum of the values of five
synchronized cycles of 5, 15, 45, 135 and 405 days, with each cycle three times
longer than the next smaller cycle and double its magnitude. Based on the time
period of the two smallest cycles, a five-day moving average was plotted three
days ahead and a 15-day moving average was plotted four days ahead. Both
moving averages were advanced in accordance with the "Square Root Rule" and
gave valid "buy" and "sell" signals in this theoretical model.

Of course, such ideally related cycles—each three times longer than the next smaller cycle, each double the magnitude of the next smaller cycle, and each having its peaks and valleys coincide timewise with a peak and valley in all smaller cycles—are not likely to be found in real life. Nevertheless, it can be seen that under ideal conditions there appears to be a definite mathematical relationship between cycles and moving averages.

Although the chart in fig. 56 utilizes closing prices only, the same principles would apply to moving average channels consisting of one moving average of the daily highs and another moving average of the daily lows.

When using moving average channels of the daily highs and daily lows, a trading rule that should be observed is: *a penetration of a moving average channel line should be considered valid only if the price has also moved beyond the previous day's range in the direction of the penetration.* Adherence to this rule will avoid some premature signals.

When moving average channels are advanced as indicated, a penetration of the moving average (and the previous day's price range) by a *single price tick* (the minimum fluctuation) should be considered a valid signal. It will almost certainly be found that there is nothing to gain by increasing the amount of the penetration required, or by rounding it off to an even number, as the probability of getting a false signal is about the same no matter how much of a penetration one selects.

Weighted Averages

The conventional method of calculating a moving average is simply to add up the prices in the series and divide by the number of prices. This gives the arithmetical mean, which is a fairly accurate representation of the average price for the period. However, since the most recent prices in the series are more representative of the current trend, it might seem logical to give more weight to those later prices. For example, in a 5-day moving average, the first price in the series could be multiplied by one, the second by two, the third by three, the fourth by four and the fifth by five. The sum would then be divided by 15 ($= 1 + 2 + 3 + 4 + 5$) to obtain a weighted 5-day average. To obtain a weighted 10-day average, the first two prices might be multiplied by one, the third and fourth prices multiplied by two, the fifth and sixth by three, etc., and the sum divided by 30. While a weighted moving average of some particular type might perhaps prove more effective than a conventional moving average in selected markets, it is also certain to have its share of false signals and whipsaws.

There is a possibility that some more sophisticated procedure, such as a moving average based on the day-to-day changes in the position of a "linear least-squares trendline" might give superior results. A linear least-squares trendline is a mathematically constructed trendline drawn through the center of a series of point-values in such a way that the sum of the squares of the differences between the line and the point-values is at a minimum. The basic formula for a least-squares trendline is:

$$Y = a + bX$$

In terms of the daily chart, "Y" is the point-value on day "X," "a" is the point-value of the line on the first day of the series (the "Y" intercept"), "b" is the slope, or the amount of advance or decline per day, and "X" is any day of the series designated by a number such as 0, 1, 2, 3, etc. The calculations for obtaining the numerical values of "a" and "b" for a linear least-squares trendline for one single brief period of say, 10 days, are quite involved and time-consuming. A simplified method for calculating "a" and "b" and the points on a linear least-squares trendline is given in Appendix B. However, with the help of an electronic calculator (or computer) that is preprogrammed for linear regression analysis, it is almost as simple as adding up the daily prices. Even then, each new daily price series must be worked up from scratch, as one cannot simply add on a new day and drop an old one, as we do with moving averages, unless all the previous day's computations have been retained in the memory of the calculator or computer.

The linear least-squares trendline is a fascinating tool, since for each price series summed up, it enables one to project a centered trendline one or more days into the future, to calculate how much of a deviation from the trendline might be expected, to obtain a "correlation coefficient" that tells how uniform or erratic the price movement is in terms of a percentage, and much more. But converting all that mathematical information into an efficient forecasting tool is not easy.

One way of doing so is to sum up a series daily—perhaps a 5-day, or a 10-day, or 20-day, or 4-week series—using closing prices only. The centered trendline is then projected one day into the future (or one week ahead in the case of a 4-week trendline), and to that price is added (or subtracted) a percentage amount equal to one-half the vertical width of the trend channel. In a bull trend the percentage would be subtracted, and in a bear trend it would be added, in order to arrive at a type of moving average that follows the trend. In the case of a 5-day or 10-day line, we would assume that the channel width is about 5% of the price, and we would add or subtract 2½% from the projected trendline price. In the case of a 20-day or 4-week trendline, the projection would be plus or minus 5%. This type of moving average will be slow to turn at the start of a move but is likely to catch the trend reversal very close to the turning point.

An interesting variation that I found to be effective in catching minor trend reversals in very volatile markets is based on a procedure quite the opposite of the one above. Instead of projecting the centered trendline ahead, I use the point of origin, or the "Y intercept" for the moving average price. A six-day linear least-squares trendline is summed up, using closing prices only, and the Y intercept, or price at point of origin, is advanced to the seventh day to be used as a moving average. As long as the trend is steep, this moving average stays far behind, but as soon as the trend slows down, the moving average comes in very close. An example of this six-day Y intercept is shown in fig. 57 (September 1976 Copper). The "buy" and "sell" prices have been circled. The inset shows the principle at work over a period of several days in detail. The day-to-day progress of the sloping 6-day centered trendline is shown as it moves through the price action.

Note how the 6-day trendline changes its slope, and bends from upward to downward as the trend turns. This type of "moving aver-

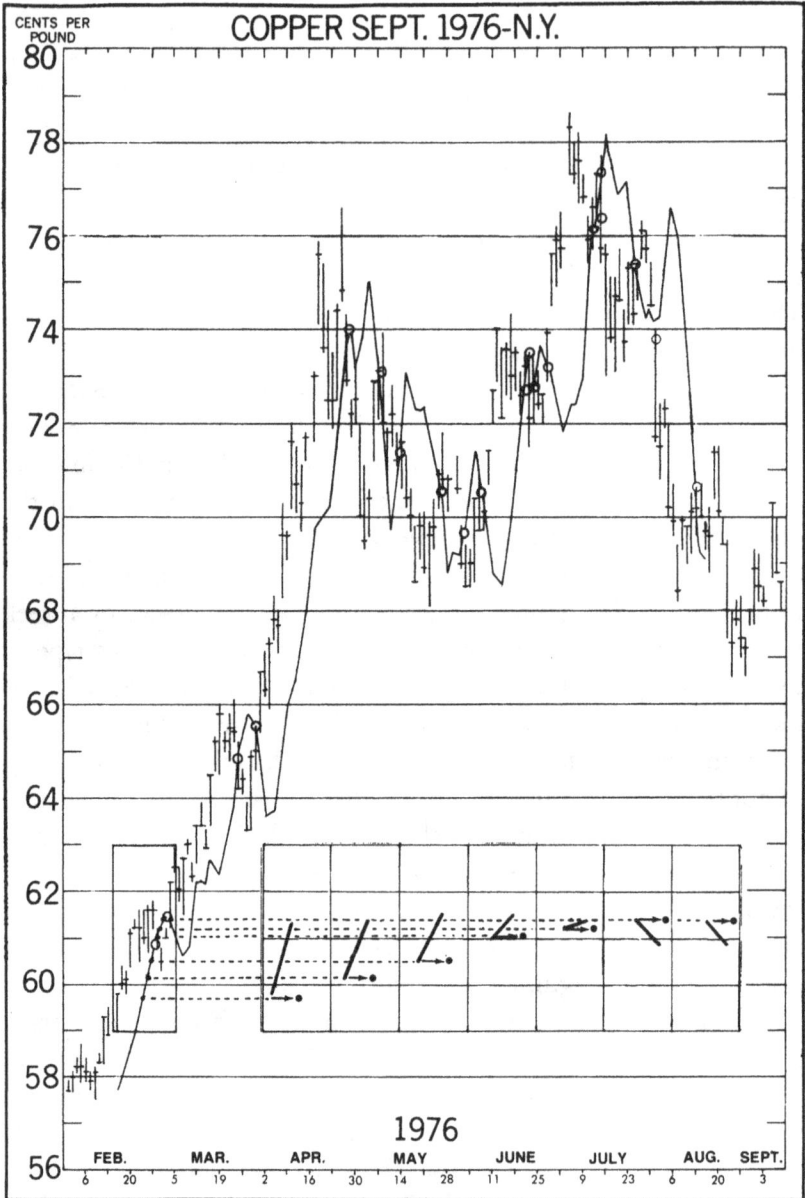

Figure 57. Minor Trend Moving Average Based on the Y-intercept of a Six-day Linear Least-squares Trendline: The inset shows the daily change in the slope of a six-day linear least-squares trendline of daily closing prices over a seven-day period. The value at the point of origin of the six-day trendline (the Y-intercept) is plotted ahead of the trend (at the seventh day) and used as a moving average. The intraday penetration of that moving average signals a reversal of trend.

age" can be extremely sensitive, catching trend reversals very close to tops and bottoms, but by the same token it is likely to whipsaw more frequently when the trend movement slows down.

In the long run, therefore, the losses from the frequent whipsaws could largely offset the greater gains from the earlier signals, and it is questionable whether this complex computer-type method would prove superior to other simpler methods.

This brings up the question of whether there actually are simple effective substitutes for moving averages and other complex computer-type methods. The answer is that if the trader finds such calculations a task he would prefer to avoid, there are indeed some excellent short-cut methods that can be quickly worked up directly from a price chart, without the need of any calculations.

Short-cut Moving Averages

There are numerous ways of simulating moving averages or substituting an effective moving line, working directly from the daily bar chart. Some methods will be described here, but the possibilities are almost endless, and the reader should not hesitate to experiment with other variations that may occur to him.

A short-term method that I have found to be effective in many fast-moving markets is one that I call a "3-day delayed stop." Essentially it uses the 3-day range to determine the stop-price for signaling a reversal of the minor trend. However, if the trend itself fails to make forward progress on any day, the forward movement of the 3-day stop is "delayed." This means that in an uptrend, as long as the daily low holds at or above the previous day's low, the sell-stop for the following day is placed just below the low of the 3-day range. However, when any day's range goes below the previous day's low, the stop-loss point cannot be advanced the next day, but must be kept at the previous day's level (until a higher bottom or double bottom is made). In a downtrend, the same procedure is followed on the downside. An example of the 3-day delayed stop is shown in Figure 58 using the same chart of September 1976 Copper.

An accepted statistical method of substituting for an arithmetical

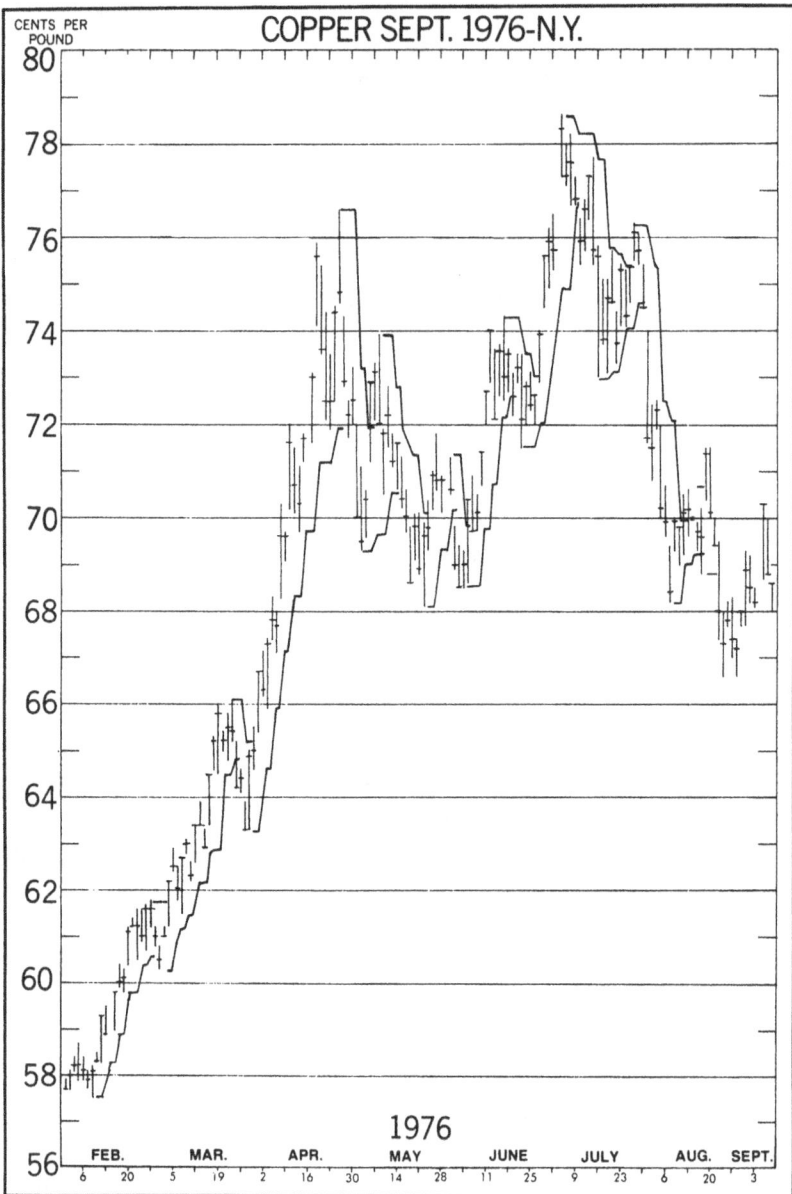

Figure 58. Short-cut Moving Average—Three-day "Delayed Stop": The moving average price for signaling a reversal of trend is the lowest price of the last three days in an uptrend and the highest price of the last three days in a downtrend. However, if the trend itself fails to move forward on any day, the forward movement of the moving average is delayed and the moving average remains unchanged until the price moves forward again. In an uptrend the progress is considered to be forward as long as the low of the latest day is at or above the low of the previous day. In a downtrend the progress is forward as long as the high of the day is at or below the high of the previous day. A trend reversal signal is given when the price penetrates the moving average.

124

mean is to use either the median number (middle value) or the mid-point between the highest and lowest values. In a 5-day moving average series the median price can be quickly determined with a glance at the price chart. To illustrate the similarity of a 5-day *moving average channel* and a 5-day *median channel*, both have been plotted on a chart of the September 1976 Copper in figs. 59 and 60. In both charts the moving averages and the moving median of the highs and the lows have been advanced three days (in accordance with the square root formula previously described.)

It is a simple matter to find quickly the median price of any 5-day price series. The two highest prices and the two lowest prices of the series are ignored, leaving the middle value to be used as the median of the five. A dot is then placed on the chart at that price level three days beyond the five-day series.

A comparison of a conventional 5-day moving average with a 5-day moving average based on the median price will show that they are very nearly the same. While the price penetrations in each will not be identical, they will probably balance out in the long run. The short-cut method also has the advantage of providing an *exact* moving average price (no decimals), leaving no doubt as to the precise critical point of penetration.

Similar results would probably be obtained if a mid-point value were used instead of a median price. One need simply count the spaces between the highest high and the lowest high of the series to obtain the mid-point moving average of the highs, and the spaces between the highest low and the lowest low of the series for the moving average low. To be really accurate, however, it would be necessary to ascertain the exact prices of those highs and lows, and divide the sum by two.

In the case of longer-term moving averages, such as 15-day, 20-day or longer, the median value or mid-point value are not as readily found as in a 5-day, 7-day or 10-day moving average. However, for longer-term moving averages other short-cuts are available. In place of a 20-day moving average channel advanced five days, one could use the *10-day range*, placing a stop-order just outside that range on the following day. The 10-day range may prove to be slightly more

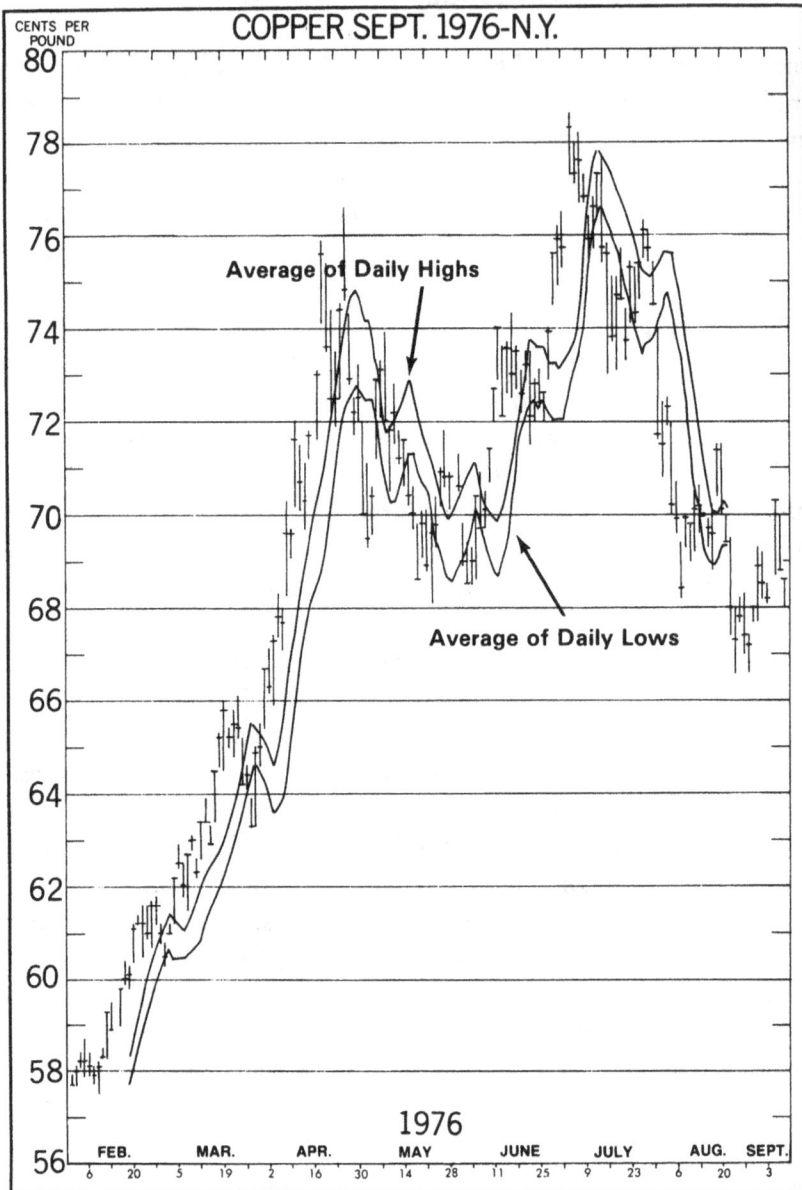

Figure 59. Five-day Moving Average Channel: A five-day moving average of the daily highs and a five-day moving average of the daily lows is calculated each day. Both moving averages are plotted three days in advance of the market. A reversal of trend is signaled when the price penetrates the moving average on the far side of the channel.

126

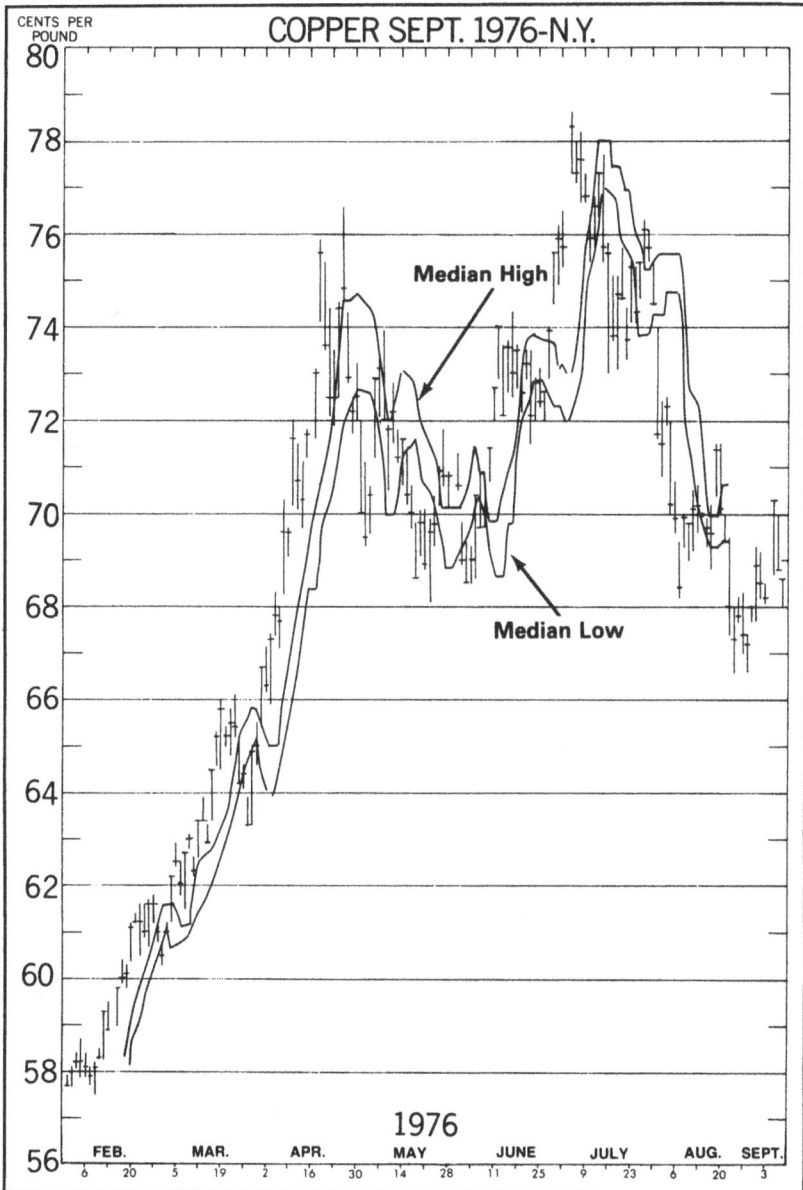

Figure 60. Short-cut Five-day Moving Average Channel Using Median Prices: Instead of calculating the five-day moving average of the daily highs and the daily lows, the median price is used for both moving averages. In a five-day series, the median price can be quickly determined by simply eliminating the two highest and two lowest prices in the series. The five-day median channel, like the moving average channel in Figure 59, is plotted three days ahead of the market. Note the similarity of the two.

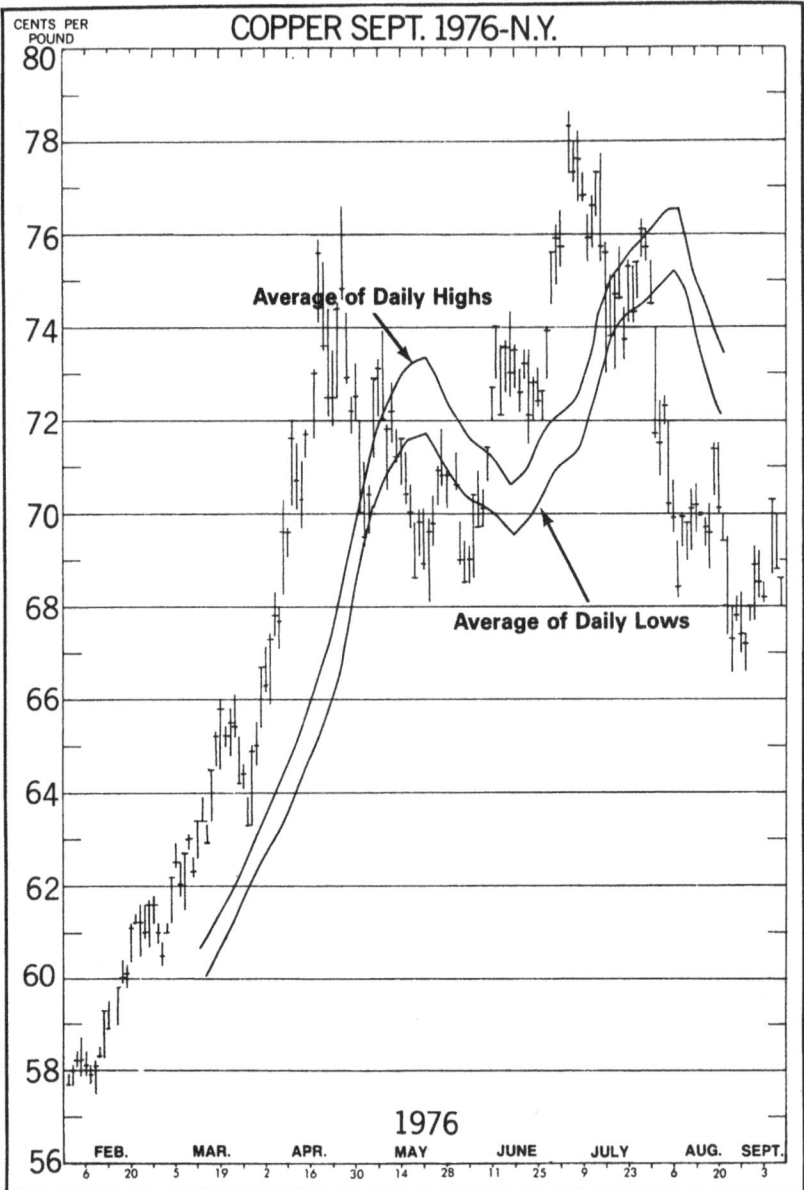

Figure 61. 20-day Moving Average Channel: In most markets the major trend can usually be defined with the help of two 20-day moving averages—one of the daily highs and one of the daily lows. The moving average channel is plotted five trading days ahead of the market. An intraday penetration through either side of the 20-day channel signals a reversal of the major trend.

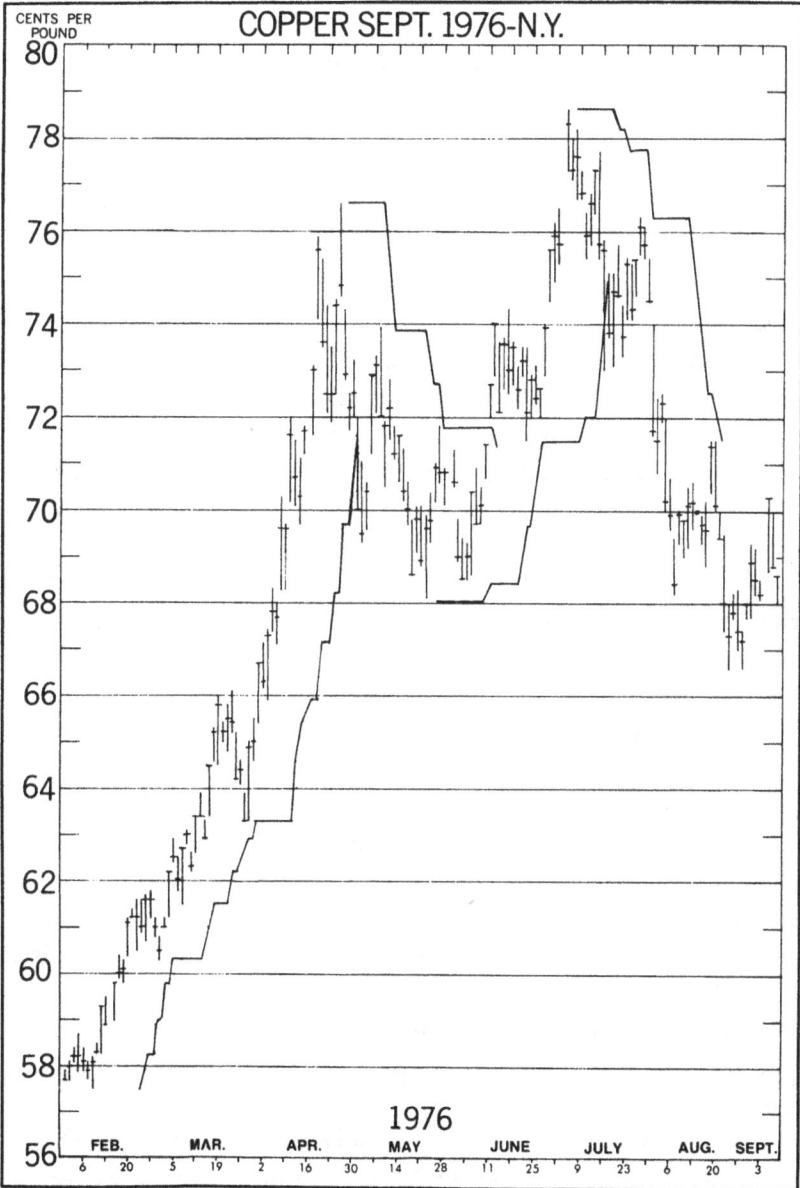

Figure 62. Short-cut Moving Average—Ten-day Range: To avoid the chore of calculating a 20-day moving average channel, a substitute moving average based on the highest (or lowest) price of the previous 10 days could be used. On this chart the 10-day range proved more accurate than the 20-day channel in Figure 61.

sensitive than the 20-day moving average channel, but will be found to be quite effective in some markets. Examples of both the 20-day moving average channel and the 10-day range are shown in figs. 61 and 62, applied to that same chart of September 1976 Copper. In this particular example, the 10-day range proved to be more accurate than the 20-day moving average, giving more meaningful signals and avoiding whipsaws.

No matter what moving average method one chooses to use, there can be no guarantee against whipsaws. The most carefully selected trend trading system will be whipsawed during prolonged flat or erratic markets. But any trading plan that is based on careful back-testing is likely to yield a good profit over reasonable periods of time. The choice of using conventional moving averages, complex weighted or computer-type moving averages, or simple short-cut methods is a matter of individual preferences, and may depend to some extent on the amount of time that can be devoted to the charts and the facilities that are available to the chartist.

Perhaps the most important point to be stressed in connection with automatic trend trading methods is the need for discipline. A trading system should be selected with great care and adopted only after the trader has good reason to feel assured that he has a potentially profitable system at hand. A substantial portion of the funds invested should be kept in reserve to absorb possible interim losses without necessitating a cutback in trading. Once the trading method has been adopted, it must be adhered to with strict discipline despite repeated whipsaws that may occur.

I have seen trend traders finish a year with substantial profits despite more than one series of repeated losses in the course of that year.

Up to now we have discussed only daily-action price charts. Longer-term charts showing weekly and monthly high-low-close information can provide a valuable longer range perspective on current price action. In the next chapter we will see how.

CHAPTER 8

Importance of Long-term Charts

Weekly Charts as a Supplement to Daily Charts

Most commodity technicians find charts showing weekly high, low, and close to be an indispensable supplement to their daily charts. A long-term chart not only gives the chartist a broader view of trends, it also enables longer term technical analysis than could possibly be applied to daily charts during their relatively short life span. Many of the techniques applicable to daily charts are equally effective when applied to weekly charts. Monthly charts must also be watched, as they give an even broader view of the market and can reinforce a chartist's long-range analysis of the weekly and daily charts.

We are referring here to weekly and monthly *continuation* charts. The term "continuation chart," as used by commodity chart technicians, has a special meaning. A weekly chart of a particular delivery month of a commodity is not a continuation chart, since it covers only the relatively short period that the contract is in existence. Once the contract expires, that weekly chart must end. A weekly "continuation chart" is plotted in accordance with any rule that permits the chartist to stop plotting an expiring contract and substitute a new one at some specified time. A continuation chart can thus have its beginning many years back, and can go on indefinitely into the future as long as trading in that commodity continues.

As with all technical chart analysis, traders should avoid giving too much weight to any conclusion drawn from a weekly chart if it is based on only a *single* chart technique. This precaution follows the Rule of Multiple Techniques described in Chapter 1, and is just as valid when analyzing weekly and monthly charts as it is with daily charts. A technique used on a weekly chart can be supported by a technique on a daily chart if both tell a similar story. For example, if a long-term support or resistance area on a weekly continuation chart coincides approximately with a measured price projection on the daily chart of the nearest delivery month, the agreement enhances the probability of their mutual accuracy. But any chart prediction based solely on one technical indicator should be viewed with skepticism.

Most weekly continuation charts show valid long-term support and resistance levels and respond well to most chart techniques, including conventional trendline treatment, most measuring techniques, zigzag trend patterns, and chart formations.

Plotting the Weekly Chart

A commodity technician should not consider his chart analysis complete unless he has taken into consideration the action shown on a weekly continuation chart as well as the action on the daily chart. If the chartist plans to keep weekly continuation charts, the question arises as to which contract month to use and what procedure to follow when switching from an expiring contract into the next nearest contract. The weekly continuation charts published by Commodity Research Bureau, Inc. as a part of their Commodity Chart Service® always show the weekly high, low, and close of the nearest delivery month. This contract is plotted until it actually expires, at which time the next nearest delivery month is "hooked on" and the chart is continued. Their weekly charts, plotted in this way, go back several years. Even though a gap and a degree of distortion may be caused by hooking on a new contract at a large discount or premium to the expiring contract, this type of chart has proved its value over the years.

If the chartist is disturbed by the distortion that can occur when switching to the next nearest delivery month, that distortion can usually be minimized by making the changeover a month or two before the nearest contract expires. During the 1950's I experimented with that idea. Although I was a subscriber to Commodity Chart Service, I also kept my own weekly charts but used the "nearby" contract instead of the expiring contract.

In constructing my own weekly continuation charts, I used the nearest delivery month, but dropped it one month *before* it became "spot." That is, if I was plotting the March contract (which becomes "spot" on March 1), I would chart it until the last trading day in January and then switch to the next nearest contract on the first trading day in February. An April contract would be plotted up to the last trading day in February, a May contract would be used until the last day of March, and so forth.

My own weekly charts, based on that "nearby" contract, sometimes showed a slightly different chart picture than Commodity Research Bureau's weekly charts, and often were less distorted at the time of switching contracts. However, I concluded that charts that used the "nearby" delivery month were not any more advantageous for purposes of chart analysis than those based on plotting the nearest delivery month to expiration. It seems that even though the nearest contract is often extremely volatile in its final days of trading, the picture it gives on a weekly chart serves effectively as a basis for technical analysis.

Analyzing Weekly Continuation Charts

Some of the techniques that are applicable to weekly charts are illustrated in figs. 63 to 76. I have chosen to emphasize trendlines and Rule-of-Seven measurements, as they appear to be especially effective on weekly charts.

Rule-of-Seven measurements can be applied to weekly charts in much the same way that they are used on the daily charts, as described in Chapter 5. It will be recalled that the size of the first "leg" of the new trend is the only information needed to calculate price objectives using the Rule of Seven. The question of whether to look for the first objective—or the second, third, or fourth—is determined largely by the *relative size* of the first leg.

As a general rule, a small initial price swing projects a third or possibly a fourth objective, while a large initial price move calls for only a first or second objective. As on the daily charts, if the first leg of a new trend on the weekly chart consists of just a few overlapping weekly ranges, the third objective or possibly the fourth is the target indicated. If the initial leg is a minor move that consists of just a few weekly ranges in a fast, steep move, the second objective may be as

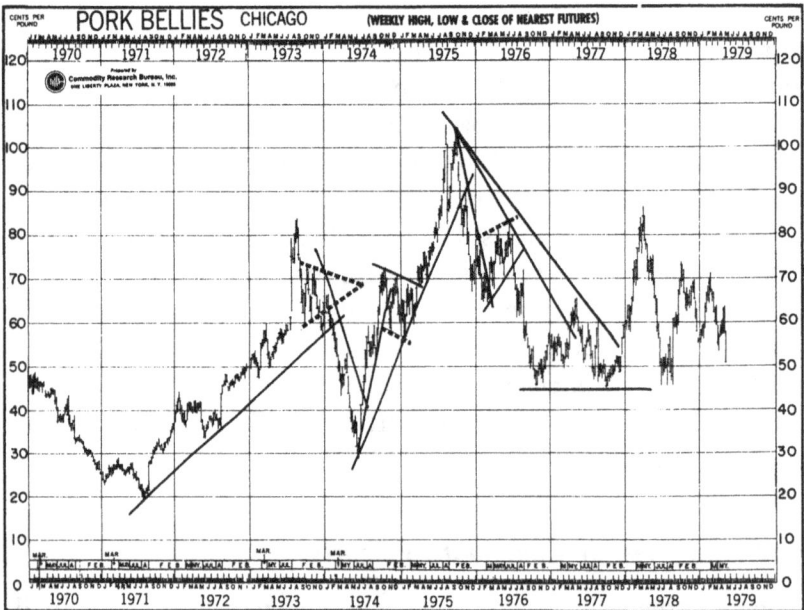

Figure 63. Weekly Pork Bellies—Trendlines: The penetration of a trendline on a weekly chart often signals an important reversal of trend. On this chart the penetration of the uptrend line in early 1974 was preceded by a downside penetration of a triangle, indicating the importance of chart formations as well. In addition to the trendline signals that were given, a bullish downward flag formation in 1974–75, when broken on the upside, signaled a new dynamic advance. A bearish upward flag in 1976 signaled the continuation of a bear trend.

far as prices will go on the next run. When the initial leg is relatively large, consisting of a series of zigzag swings, the next move will usually carry only to the first objective. These are all relative comparisons, and one must learn to use judgment, tempered by experience, when setting a target. Rule-of-Seven measurements, like all other technical indicators, should be confirmed by one or more other technical indicators.

Now let's examine a few weekly charts.

Pork Bellies

If one had been watching the weekly chart of Pork Bellies prior to 1973, a trendline could have been drawn upward from the 1971 low just under 20¢ and through the 1972 dip around 35¢. It would have been reconfirmed in late December 1973, as shown in fig. 63, by the bounce from about 56½¢. That uptrend line was penetrated in February, 1974 with bearish consequences. Just below the 1973 peak, prices paused for several weeks in a converging triangular pattern that was broken downside in December, hinting at the eventual penetration of the uptrend line. Referring for a moment to the same chart in fig. 64, note that the downside penetration of the triangle low enabled the chartist to make a measurement by the Rule of Seven. Since the initial down leg from the 84¢ peak, although very steep, consisted of only a single downswing of about five weeks, a "minor" type measurement could be made to a second or third objective, both of which proved valid.

The V-bottom in 1974 was characteristically abrupt, and would have been difficult to recognize as a major bottom except for the fact that a downtrend line across the 1973–74 decline was penetrated in July following the achievement of the third Rule-of-Seven target. A steep uptrend line from the 1974 low was broken in November of that year, but as 1975 began it became evident that a potentially bullish downward-waving flag formation was taking shape. The upside breakout from that flag at about 68¢ in late March gave a bull signal, which was further confirmed when prices rose above the top of the flag at about 72½¢. It was then time to draw a new uptrend line and

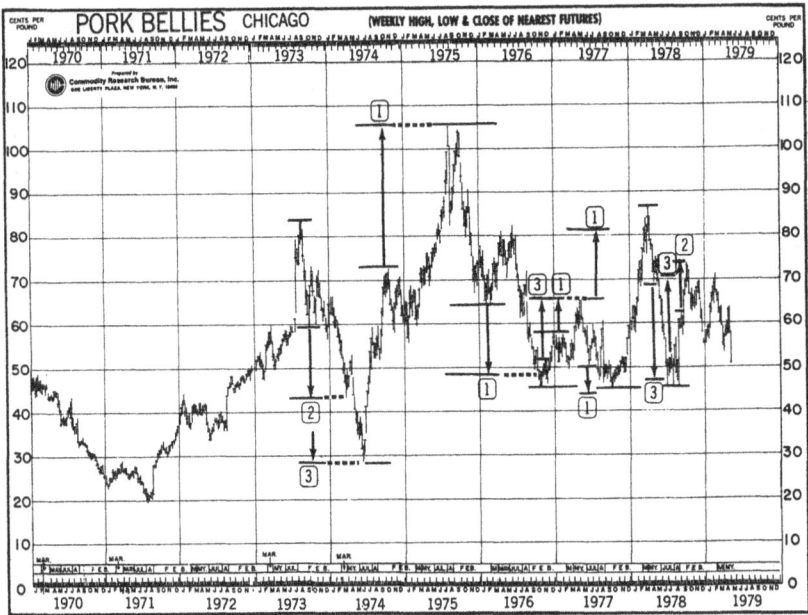

Figure 64. Weekly Pork Bellies—Rule of Seven: Rule of Seven measurements often give accurate projections on the weekly charts. The rules for projecting such measurements are the same as those used for the daily charts. Some first, second, and third objectives are shown here, all of which proved quite accurate in their predictions.

to look for some upside measurements. Since a flag formation often occurs at the halfway point of a price move, one could have taken a swing measurement to the 98½¢ area and a Rule-of-Seven measure to the first objective around $1.05 with obvious success.

A narrow double top then formed at about $1.05, followed by a bearish break of both the uptrend line and the intervening low just above 82¢. A potentially bearish upward-waving flag that took form during the first half of 1976 was penetrated downside at the end of June. That downside action paved the way for a Rule-of-Seven measurement to 48½¢. The four-week rally from the 1976 low of 45.60¢ gave a third objective of 66.07¢ which was supported by a first objective of 66.42¢ measured upward from the 57.50¢ peak of February, 1977. The actual peak reached in May was 65.65¢. From that peak the big five-week decline to 50.85¢ gave a first downside objective of 44.93¢, a close match to the actual low of 45.40¢ in October, 1977.

When the price moved up through the high of 65.65¢ a double bottom formation was completed and an upside projection could be made. The first objective measurement gave a target of 80.84¢, in the area of the old 1976 high. The steep advance carried to 86.25¢ before turning back. The brief four-week decline from that 1978 high could be utilized to measure a third downside objective to 47.16¢, suggesting that the market might be heading back to the old double bottom, which was exactly what did happen. During July and August of 1978 the price bounced from the 45.50¢ area three times and then headed upward. The first small rally to 52.92¢ gave a third objective of 71.24¢, while the second and more extensive rally to 56.75¢ gave a second objective of 71.71¢. Both measurements were around the level of the small resistance area that formed in April-May 1978 and closely matched the October, 1978 peak of 73.70¢.

Soybeans

When soybeans came tumbling down from their 1973 historic high of $12.90, the weekly chart (figs. 65 and 66) did not provide any price targets that could confirm each other. However, after the rally in the first quarter of 1974 had been completed, it could be seen that a downtrend line from the historic peak caught the upturn virtually at the bottom, near $5.50. The subsequent advance to about $9.55 went somewhat beyond the second Rule-of-Seven objective of $9.00. The peak, however, at $9.55, was made in the large gap area that occurred on the way down in 1973.

The uptrend line across the 1974 lows caught the downturn nicely, and the four-week decline of the first leg gave a Rule-of-Seven (third) downside objective around $5.00—a fairly accurate assessment.

Then some interesting developments occurred. In the first quarter of 1975, after reaching the downside objective, prices rallied and then fell back to the $5.00 area before turning upward again. This completed a small double bottom, which gave a false promise of bullishness. There was a minor three-week upswing from the second low of that double bottom that could have been utilized for an up-

Figure 65. Weekly Soybeans—Trendlines: Despite the wild and erratic long-term price swings in this market, trendlines provided an excellent means of calling the trend reversals.

side measurement to at least a third objective, which was promptly reached and exceeded. It looked as though the bullish promise was about to be fulfilled. But the market turned down instead and went through the old lows.

A new downtrend line across the 1974–75 peaks could then have been drawn, the upside penetration of which signaled the start of a new bull move early in 1976. The first small upleg from the $4.40 low would have given a fourth upside objective above $8.00, but there was too much overhead resistance at the 1974 congestion area around $7.50 to permit a further price climb. This first major upleg, however, could have been used for projecting an upside target of about $10.00, which proved to be in the general area of the 1977 top.

It was then time to draw an uptrend line across the 1976 lows. The downside penetration of that uptrend line in 1977 gave a very late signal, but it was a valid one. There was actually no clear initial downleg to use for a Rule-of-Seven measurement. There was an upside reversal, however, after the first three weeks of decline from the top, and one could use that distance from $10.76½ to $9.13½ as the

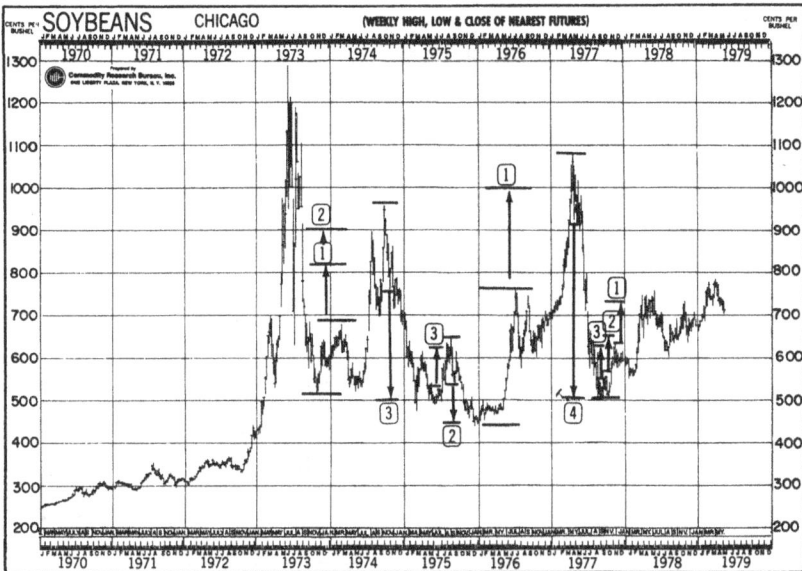

Figure 66. Weekly Soybeans—Rule of Seven: There were numerous opportunities to set up long-term Rule of Seven objectives here. As can be seen, most of the measurements gave helpful indications of target areas.

basis for a possible fourth objective to $5.06, since it happened to coincide with the 1975–76 support zone. The 1977 bear trend made a bottom at exactly that price!

From the low of $5.06 the market rallied twice and fell back each time to the lows before starting up. The first small one-week rally to $5.46 gave a third objective of $6.46. The second small upswing to $5.69 gave a second objective of $6.52¾. The actual November, 1977 peak was $6.34½. When the upturn in the first quarter of 1978 took out that November high it was time to take measurements and to estimate the possible extent of the next advance. The first objective was $7.31, which proved to be reasonably close to the multiple peaks around $7.50.

Soybean Oil

Conventional trendlines applied to the weekly Soybean Oil chart proved to be quite meaningful during the mid-1970's. Almost every penetration of a trendline was followed by a substantial price move

Figure 67. Weekly Soybean Oil—Trendlines: Conventional trendlines applied to this weekly chart proved to be quite meaningful during the 1970's. Almost every penetration of a trendline was followed by a significant price move in the direction indicated.

in the direction signaled. The up and down trends were also fairly well defined in terms of the zigzag swings of prices. There were ascending highs and lows during extended uptrends, and descending highs and lows when the main trend pointed downward. Although there were not many opportunities to apply Rule-of-Seven measurements, the most obvious ones are shown in fig. 68. The first objective measurements were based on zigzag upswings that could be classified as "major" initial up-legs, while the third objective targets were projected from "minor" initial legs of just a few weeks. The downturn from the 1977 high does not seem to lend itself readily to a Rule-of-Seven measurement. However, the support area around 16¢–18¢ could be expected to block the decline and to serve as a downside target.

The rally from the October 1977 low of 17.27¢ to the December 1977 high of 24.00¢ was the first leg of a new uptrend and could be

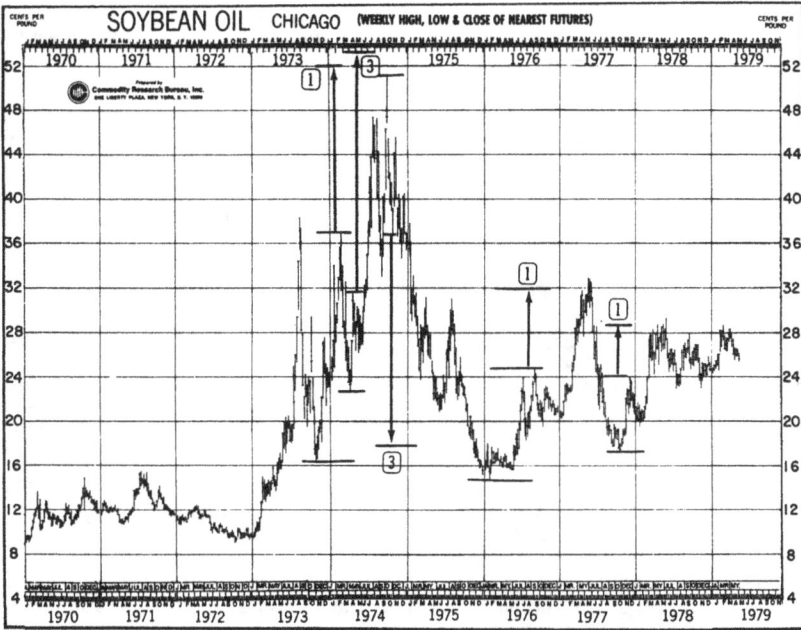

Figure 68. Weekly Soybean Oil—Rule of Seven: There were not many opportunities to apply Rule of Seven measurements to this weekly chart, but on the few occasions it could be used the projections were reasonably accurate.

used to project a first objective of 29.05¢. That target price was closely matched by the actual peak of 29.30¢ made on May 31, 1978. The decline from that peak ruptured an uptrend line across the lows of October, 1977 and February, 1978, and hinted at a possible decline ahead. A downtrend line across the 1978 peaks was penetrated upside, but prices backed away from previous highs, leaving the outlook uncertain.

Live Hogs

In the many years covered by the weekly chart of Live Hogs (fig. 69), very few major trendlines could be drawn. During the uptrend from the 1974 low, the dips in September and November lined up so perfectly with the low point that no chartist could be blamed for drawing an initial uptrend line through those three points. The

Figure 69. Weekly Live Hogs—Trendlines: In the many years covered by this weekly chart only a few trendlines could be drawn. Some of them proved premature, as indicated by the dotted lines. However, premature trendlines can sometimes be helpful when extended into the future. An example is the premature uptrend line drawn from the 1974 low. When extended upward it became a line of overhead resistance that obstructed the 1975 advance.

downside penetration of that line in January, 1975 proved false, however, and after two months of relatively trendless action prices resumed their upward journey. The initial trendline is shown as a dotted line, and it has been extended upward to the top of the chart to demonstrate a function that broken initial trendlines sometimes serve. A trendline that is penetrated prematurely, if extended into the future, often acts as a barrier to subsequent price movement. In this example, the initial uptrend line blocked the advance in June, July, and September, 1975.

In fig. 70 some Rule-of-Seven measurements are shown on the same chart of Live Hogs. In accordance with the general rules previously described, if an initial leg of the new trend was relatively large a first objective was projected; if the initial leg was relatively small, a third objective was projected; and, an initial leg of relatively moderate size was given a second objective. Note that after the initial "minor" decline from the 1975 top there was a rally in Novem-

Figure 70. Weekly Live Hogs—Rule of Seven: Initial price swings of large magnitude were used to project a first objective, while initial swings of lesser magnitude were used to project second or third objectives. All the targets shown here proved to be reasonably accurate in their forecasts.

ber that formed a small right shoulder in a head-and-shoulders top. The 15¢ decline from the head to the neckline, projected an equal distance downward from the neckline, gave a minimum downside target of 35¢, and thereby added its confirmation to the two Rule-of-Seven targets slightly below. The initial up-leg from the 1976 low is neither very small nor very large, and suggests an advance to a first objective of 50½¢ and a second objective at about 57½¢, both of which were satisfied.

Plywood

On the weekly Plywood chart (fig. 71) the ascending highs and ascending lows during 1975–77 form a clearly bullish upward zigzag pattern. The uptrend line across the 1975–76 lows appears to be a valid long-term trendline, the penetration of which brought the three-year uptrend to a halt. The zigzag swings that make up the long-term uptrend all have their own short-term zigzag movements

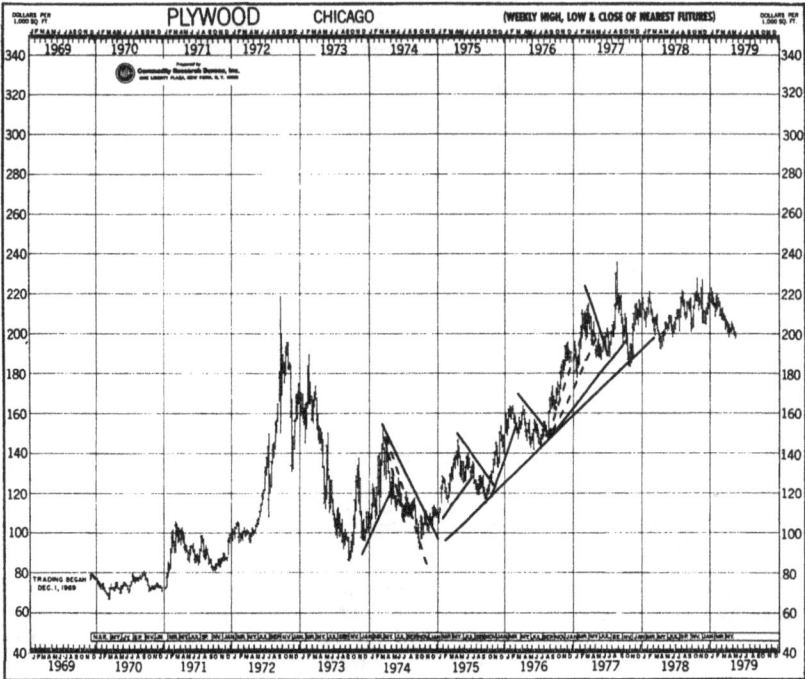

Figure 71. Weekly Plywood—Trendlines: Both long-term and short-term trendlines could be drawn on this chart. Some short-term trendlines proved premature
and had to be redrawn. A typical fan formation developed in 1974 when two
downtrend lines were falsely penetrated. The third trendline proved valid and
signaled the start of a prolonged bull move.

and their own trendlines. Some premature penetrations of short-term
trendlines are apparent, with the 1974 downtrend lines forming a
three-line fan, in which the penetration of the third downtrend line
proved valid.

In fig. 72 some Rule-of-Seven measurements are shown. When the
peaks of 1974 and 1975 were exceeded early in 1976, it signaled the
probable start of a long-term advance. At that time it was appropriate to project a long-range first objective and possibly a second, based
on the initial advance from the 1973 low to the 1974 high. This gave
a first upside target of $206, which was satisfied early in 1977; and, a
possible second upside target around $244. Since a very small initial
leg can project a fourth objective, the two-week advance from the
1974 low could be used for that purpose. Note that its fourth objec-

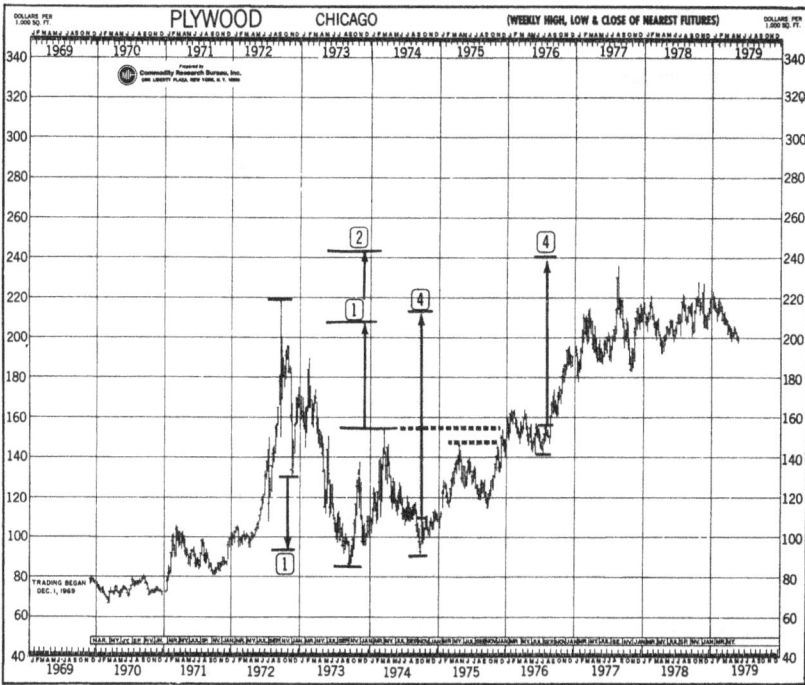

Figure 72. Weekly Plywood—Rule of Seven: The prolonged uptrend from the 1973 low gave very few opportunities for Rule of Seven measurements. However, those measurements that could be made predicted an extensive advance that was fully confirmed by the subsequent action.

tive measurement, at about $211, coincided approximately with the first major upside objective at $206, both of which predicted the area of the March 1977 top. A similar fourth upside measurement can be projected from the initial three-week advance from the July 1976 low, which projects a target of about $240—pretty much in line with second major upside target of $244. The actual high of $236 fell somewhat short of those two long-term objectives.

Cotton

Looking at the trendlines on the weekly Cotton chart in fig. 73, it is immediately obvious that there were false penetrations made during the 1974 decline, the 1975 advance, and the 1976 downturn. In

Figure 73. Weekly Cotton—Trendlines: Here is an unusual example of three successive fan formations. Two premature trendlines followed by a third and valid trendline were evident in the 1974 decline, the 1975–76 advance, and the 1976–77 decline.

all three cases, however, the trendline patterns made fairly typical "fan" formations, with two successive trendlines that were prematurely penetrated followed by a third and valid trendline. In "fan" formations like these, the chartist must not become so frustrated by the first two whipsaws that he fails to recognize the importance of the third penetration.

The Rule-of-Seven measurements shown in fig. 74 proved quite valid. The initial downturn from the 99¢ peak in 1973 was a dynamic decline that took about five weeks. Although it was a straight drop with no important rally, it could hardly be classified as a "minor" downswing and therefore could not justify a downside projection to a third or fourth objective. At the same time, the lack of zigzag swings within that decline prevented it from being classified as a "major" downswing, which would normally project to a

Figure 74. Weekly Cotton—Rule of Seven: Most of the measurements shown coincided with important tops or bottoms. An exception was the 1973 advance, which was a rare case of a relatively large initial upswing projecting to a third objective rather than to a first or second objective. Perhaps in the light of history that initial upswing could now be viewed as "minor" in magnitude.

first objective. A second objective would therefore appear to be the winner by default.

This second objective gave a downside target around about 41¢, which was slightly exceeded by the 36½¢ low. The downside measurement to a first objective (which was ruled out above) actually coincided with a small congestion area in the low 50's, from which level the market did bounce, giving the false upside penetration of the second downtrend line. This was admittedly a case of multiple techniques giving the wrong answer—one of the rare instances in which I have seen the Rule of Multiple Techniques fail.

However, the third downtrend line across the 1974 bear trend caught the 1975 upturn very near the bottom, after having satisfied the second downside objective. The very small initial upswing to

Figure 75. Weekly Corn—Trendlines: The massive top formation that was in progress from 1973 to 1976 did not permit many meaningful trendlines to be drawn. During that period prices bounced three times from the $2.45–$2.50 area. When that vital support area was ruptured late in 1976, it signaled the start of a major downtrend.

40½¢ justified projecting a fourth upside objective to the 64¢ area, which coincided with an important top. The resumption of the up-trend early in 1976 gave a first upside objective in the low 80's, which coincided almost exactly with a measured swing objective. The runaway bull market overshot those targets but quickly fell back. In any event, the projected advance to the low 80's served notice that a substantial price climb could follow the upside penetration of the small double top around 63¢. The first downleg in 1976 was similar in character to the initial decline from the 1973 top, and implied a decline to a second objective in the area of 54¢, which was reached and exceeded. The final low for the move was 49.10¢, reached in December, 1977. The irregular advance from that low did not form any well-defined initial up-leg from which to make a mea-

Figure 76. Weekly Corn—Rule of Seven: The three-year top formation permitted very few Rule of Seven measurements to be made. When the 1975 low was penetrated late in 1976 it called for a major downswing to a first objective around $1.87, which seemed quite far away at the time. Unattainable as it may have seemed, it was soon satisfied by an actual low of $1.80½.

surement. However, there were two "minor" upswings that could be used. The first was the three-week advance to 54.55¢, which came to a halt on December 30 and fell back for one week. A third objective measurement based on that brief upswing projected to 68.17¢. The second small upswing was the nine-week advance from 49.10¢ to 57.05¢. A Rule-of-Seven first objective called for a target around 63.01¢, with a second objective at 67.62¢. The May peak of 62.70¢ and the October 30 peak of 70.70¢ appear to have satisfied those objective measurements.

Corn

In fig. 75, the trendlines on the weekly Corn chart are self-explanatory. This was a period during which a massive top was forming, with long-term trend direction still lacking. Trendlines within that broad top were therefore not as meaningful as they might otherwise have been. During 1974 and 1975, prices bounced three times from the $2.45–2.50 area. That vital support was ruptured decisively in the last quarter of 1976, signaling the start of a major bear trend.

In fig. 76 some Rule-of-Seven measurements are shown, including the first downside target of the bear trend which projected to the $1.87 area. The first two measurements shown are "minor" swing targets projected to a third and fourth objective. From the 1977 low of $1.80½ prices moved up and consolidated for many weeks under a high of $2.28½. The resumption of the advance in March, 1978 permitted a first objective measurement to be projected to $2.64½.

Trading Off the Weekly Charts

Since weekly continuation charts are kept by switching from an expiring contract into the next nearest contract, often at a substantial difference in price, one cannot trade off the weekly charts in the same way one trades off the daily charts. Technical analysis of a weekly continuation chart must always be made with the realization that resulting forecasts can be applied only to the actual delivery month that is to be plotted on the chart at some later date. A trendline on a weekly continuation chart could possibly be broken simply by hooking on the new contract. An upside or downside objective that seems relatively far off might possibly be achieved overnight at the time of switching into the next contract. In an extremely "inverted" market (one in which each delivery month is at a price premium to the next later delivery month), a conventional weekly continuation chart could show a downtrend when in fact the individual months, which have been overdiscounted, keep moving up in bull trends. This has actually happened in the past, one example being the New York Cocoa market in 1974-75. In the first week of May, 1974 the expiring May contract peaked out at a then-record high of 109.50¢. At that time all later delivery months were trading at big discounts to the expiring May. As the July, September, and December contracts were hooked on, prices kept zigzagging downward on the weekly continuation chart. The daily charts, however, continued to show upward trends during that same period. The December 1974 contract, which had made a contract high of 81.80¢ at the time the old expiring May contract hit that 109.50¢ peak, subsequently climbed to a new high of 91.05¢ in time to be hooked on to the weekly chart as one of a series of lower tops within the apparent downtrend on that chart.

Based on the weekly Cocoa continuation chart, a downtrend was already in progress, yet a long position would have been the correct one to hold for a while longer. Weekly continuation charts must therefore be used primarily as a supplement to the daily charts, and only rarely as a basis for specific trading action.

Making Use of a Weekly Index Chart

If the chartist feels the need for a weekly chart that reflects the true size and direction of each major price swing, without the distortion that can be caused by the hooking on of a new contract at a different price level, he can plot a "Weekly Index Chart" of the commodity to be traded.

On an Index Chart, when a new contract is hooked on *the price is adjusted to offset the difference between the prices of the old and new contracts.* There are various ways in which an Index Chart of this type could be devised. Since most traders rarely take a position in the nearest delivery month of a commodity during the last few weeks of its life, the Weekly Index Chart would probably serve its purpose best if based on the second nearest contract rather than the nearest contract. The plan would be to switch out of the "nearby" contract on the Index Chart one month before it becomes "spot," as explained earlier in this chapter. That "nearby" contract is usually the one with the largest open interest, and is therefore usually the most liquid contract. It is also likely to be most representative of the market for purposes of chart analysis.

When "hooking on" the new contract, *a price adjustment is made to offset the prevailing spread differential.* This price adjustment could be made in a variety of ways. One way is to base it on the difference between the *average* of the weekly high, low, and close of the expiring contract and the average of the incoming contract during the week just completed. Each time a new contract is hooked on, the new differential must be added to the sum of all previous differentials. A continuing record must be kept of both the latest switch difference and the cumulative total.

For example, suppose we were making an Index Chart of Plywood futures. The delivery months traded are January, March, May, July, September and November. If we had decided to start that Index Chart in the first week of January, 1978 we would have used the prices of the March 1978 contract during January. Since we had just started the chart, Index prices and the actual prices would be identical. The last full week in January, 1978 ended on January 27. On that Friday, after the close of the market, we would calculate the Index factor to be used on the incoming May contract.

To obtain that Index factor we take the *weekly* high, low, and closing prices of the outgoing March contract, which were $213.30, $207.90, $212.40, and find the average, which was $211.20. We do the same with the incoming May contract, whose weekly high, low, and closing prices were $214.90, $209.60, $213.90, for an average of $212.80. Based on those average prices, the incoming May contract was trading at a premium of $1.60 over March. In order to line up the incoming May contract with the outgoing March contract, we must subtract the difference of $1.60 from the May prices. The Index factor during February and March (when the May contract is used) will be "minus $1.60." Each week during that two-month period we will take the weekly high, low, and closing prices of the May contract and subtract $1.60 to obtain the high, low, and closing prices of the Index.

The next change in the Index factor would be made after the close in the last week of March, when we must switch from the May contract into the July contract. During that week the high, low, and close of the May contract averaged $198.20 and the incoming July contract averaged $200.10. The difference of the old contract minus the new contract gave a factor of minus $1.90, which must now be added to the previous factor of minus $1.60, resulting in a cumulative factor of minus $3.50. Therefore, to arrive at the correct Index prices during April and May we must subtract $3.50 from the weekly high, low, and closing prices of the July contract.

At the end of May the incoming September contract, instead of being at a premium to the outgoing July contract, was now at a discount. The average prices in the last week of May were $206.20 for the July contract and $201.40 for the September contract. The difference in this instance was plus $4.80 which, when added to the previous cumulative factor of minus $3.50, gave a new cumulative factor of plus $1.30. To line up the incoming September contract with the Index during June and July, it would be necessary to add the new cumulative factor of plus $1.30 to the weekly high, low, and closing prices of the September contract. At the end of each two-month period a new cumulative factor would be obtained in the same way and would be applied to the incoming contract to arrive at the Index prices for that period.

In Plywood there are six delivery months, each two months apart. Most other commodities have a different series of delivery months, and the length of time each new incoming contract will be used for the Index Chart might vary from one month to several months. Each commodity would change its factor at its own appropriate time intervals, depending on the delivery months used in that commodity.

When projecting price trends or price objectives on an Index Chart of this type it is a simple matter to convert projected Index prices back to real market prices based on the cumulative factor then in use.

If a market goes through a prolonged period of relatively trendless action, during which time the nearest delivery month is always at a discount to the later delivery months, the Index Chart is likely to show more of a downward trend than the regular weekly continuation chart. As each far-off delivery month becomes "spot" it will tend to lose its premium and come down toward the lower level of the "spot" market. If a major upturn later takes place, the Index Chart is likely to show a much greater price advance than the weekly continuation chart. After a substantial price advance there is usually a tendency for the futures market to become "inverted." That is, the nearest contract is likely to be at a premium, with all later delivery months at successively larger discounts to the nearest contract. The result would be that when the bull market finally comes to an end the later delivery months will already have been trading at the lower levels for some time. The weekly continuation chart would therefore "hook on" each new contract at a big discount, showing a substantial decline as a result, while the Index Chart might show only a sideways movement or perhaps even an advance. For showing profit potential, the Index Chart would probably be more realistic.

The actual total price movement that a trader could attempt to capture by switching ahead as each nearby contract approached maturity might be considerably greater or considerably less than the apparent price move as shown on the weekly continuation chart. Whether the actual major price move was greater or less would depend largely on whether the later delivery months were lagging behind the trend or anticipating it.

During the late 1950's I decided to plot Weekly Continuation Charts and Weekly Index Charts of several commodities. Among the commodities I charted were Chicago Eggs and Winnipeg Flaxseed. In the Egg market at that time contract months were September, October, November, December, and January. When the January contract expired each year, the next nearest delivery month was always the distant September contract, which was usually priced at a big premium to the expiring January.

On the weekly continuation chart of Eggs, prices had a tendency to move downward throughout each year, only to leap back to previous high levels when the September contract was hooked on in January. On my Index Chart of Chicago Eggs, this seasonal distortion was eliminated, and the bearish long-term trading trend was revealed.

On the Egg weekly continuation chart, despite the big annual upswing, prices eventually came down from a high of about 48¢ in January, 1955 to a low of about 21½¢ in January, 1960—an apparent long-term decline of 26½¢. In that same period of time, my Index Chart of Chicago Eggs (mainly because of the consistent premium of the September contract) declined a total of 43¢—from a high of 48¢ to a low of 5¢! Furthermore, even though the 21½¢ low on the weekly continuation chart proved to be the bottom on that chart, the price on the Index Chart, after a brief rally, fell to a new low that year, declining below the one-cent level!

The Egg Index Chart showed that in terms of realistic price change the actual total profit potential on the short side of that market for that period of time was almost double the amount that was indicated on the weekly continuation chart.

A similar development in the opposite direction took place in the Winnipeg Flaxseed market. On the weekly continuation chart, Winnipeg Flax moved up from a low of about $2.35 in 1957 to a high of about $4.12 in 1959—an advance of about $1.77. On the Index Chart of Winnipeg Flaxseed, the price climbed from a low of $2.39 to a high of $4.45, an advance of $2.06. Here too, the upside profit potential proved to be much greater than indicated by the price changes in the nearest contract on a weekly continuation chart.

Because of the added perspective it gives, a weekly Index Chart can often be a helpful supplement to the regular weekly continuation charts, if the chartist has the time and the inclination to plot those additional charts.

It's time now for me to recap—and, in the process, to add a few words about trading volume and open interest.

CHAPTER **9**

Summing It Up

A commodity trader with a knowledge of chart techniques has a distinct advantage over the trader with little or no familiarity with price charts. An understanding of the nature of price movements enables the chart technician to trade on the basis of a well-prepared plan that can help to maximize profits and keep risks under control. However, there is no trading plan that will yield a profit on every trade. No matter what approach one takes to the market, there can be no guarantee that prices will not move in the wrong direction after a position has been taken. The best one can hope to accomplish is for gains to exceed losses over a reasonable period of time. This can be achieved if the trader is willing and able to devote some time every day to the study and analysis of the markets he is following.

To be successful, a commodity trader must have a plan of action that shows promise of yielding net profits in the future based on a record of the past. When setting up such a plan, it must be kept in mind that there is much random price movement within basic trends, and the trader must either find some way to take advantage of those random price swings or make due allowance for the possibility of counterswings that can occur without apparent reason within a trend.

There are countless approaches to commodity trading, and each trader

must find for himself the plan that appears to be best suited to his individ-
ual circumstances and temperament.

If one prefers to lean heavily on fundamental analysis as a guide to upside or downside potential, he would still do well to utilize price chart analysis for help in timing his market commitments and keeping his risks under control. This advice applies to both commercial hedge traders and to speculators. The trader who relies primarily on his price charts must make a choice between automatic trend trading and trading off the charts with the use of various techniques based on personal judgment.

Automatic Trend Trading

For the trader who prefers to follow automatic "buy" and "sell" signals, there are many approaches. The simplest, of course, is to follow faithfully a computer trend service such as the daily Electronic Futures Trend Analyzer offered by Commodity Research Bureau, Inc.; or, to put your account under the control of a person or firm operating such a service. It is not the purpose of this book to recommend any specific automatic trend-trading methods, but merely to describe a few promising techniques that might serve as a guide for setting up a sophisticated program of one's own.

One could also make use of the zigzag swings of the minor trend based on the day-to-day movement of prices, as described in Chapter 2. Moving averages could be used in a variety of ways, a few of which were suggested in Chapter 7. A daily-net-change oscillator could be used, as described in Chapter 6, to determine when and where to draw a meaningful minor trendline. Two or more trading methods could be used in conjunction with each other, either to confirm each other or to establish both major and minor trend signals.

The markets to be traded should be selected on the basis of good response in the past to the particular trading method to be used. While it is preferable to have the automatic trading method in each market specially tailored to fit that market, some trading methods may give reasonably good performance over a broad spectrum of markets. If the trader intends to concentrate on just a few markets, the techniques that fit those markets best are the ones to use. If many markets are to be traded, it may be necessary to compromise by settling on a single good trading plan for all. If a single standard trading method for all markets is to be used, it should be selected carefully after exhaustive back-testing, and allowance should be made for relatively poor performance at times in some markets.

A trader must be self-disciplined. Once an automatic trading system has been decided upon, it should be followed rigidly. The automatic trend trader must be prepared to accept the whipsaws that will inevitably occur from time to time, as well as the substantial profits that will usually result from the occasional extended price moves.

Trading off the Charts

Not everyone is comfortable with automatic trend trading. Many chart technicians prefer to simply trade "off the charts," using their knowledge of chart techniques as a basis for their trading decisions. Both approaches require considerable homework, the exact amount depending on how many markets are to be followed and how many different techniques are employed.

When trading off the charts, it is important to review the status of weekly and monthly charts frequently. Among the important things to look for on the long-term continuation charts are major support and resistance areas, major trendlines, classic chart formations, and Rule-of-Seven measurements. If the long-term charts being used are based on the nearest delivery month (as they usually are), allowance must be made on the daily charts for the difference in relationship between the nearest delivery month and the actual contract being traded. If a weekly "Index Chart" is available, it should be analyzed in the same way as the regular continuation chart. If seasonal tendencies are prominent in a market, they should also be taken into consideration.

On the daily charts one must look at the zigzag swings of the market, and since there are many trends going on at the same time, one must determine at all times which trend he is trading. A broad view of the market should be taken first, with an eye to price formations such as head-and-shoulders tops or bottoms, triangle formations, multiple tops and bottoms, large flag formations, and slope formations. The critical levels of trendlines and Predicted Trendlines should be noted, as should the positions of two or three different-sized curved channels.

For a closer look at the trend, watch for small drift patterns as a key to near-term trend direction. Use conventional trendlines and the various Predicted Trendlines as a help in timing trades. Try to apply every possible objective measurement listed in Chapter 5. Above all, keep in mind the Rule of Multiple Techniques. Discard isolated chart signals that are not supported by other signals or techniques. Set up a "check list" of things to look for and evaluate. The list does not have to be all-inclusive, but should include those techniques in which the trader has the most confidence. The check-list might look something like this:

Long-term Continuation Charts:
1. Support and resistance areas.
2. Trendlines.
3. Chart Formations.
4. Rule-of-Seven measurements.

Daily Charts:
1. Zigzag trend patterns—minor and major.
2. Classic chart formations, especially large and small "drift" patterns.
3. Trendlines and Predicted Trendlines, with special emphasis on Reaction Predicted Trendlines.
4. Curved trend channels, each double the vertical width of the next smaller one.
5. Upside or downside objectives measured by support and resistance areas, head-and-shoulders, triangle and slope measurements, swing and counterswing measurements, 50% reaction, midway gaps, Rule-of-Seven, and 17–35 measurements.

Although your trading would be based solely on your own judgment of the market, you could, if you wish, include the use of one or more moving averages, a net-change oscillator, or any other mechanical device to be evaluated with discretion along with your other technical "tools."

Short Term "In-and-Out" Trading

It cannot be repeated too often that the key to profits in commodity trading is identification of trend direction. The price move that one trades might be the trend of an hour, a day, a month, or a year, but to successfully buy low and sell high a trader *must* ride a trend. It is certainly very gratifying to put on a position at the start of a new trend and to liquidate it days, weeks, or months later at a substantial profit after the trend has run its course. For most traders, however, some of the reactions that occur during the course of a trend are a source of worry and frustration. Unrealized gains can suddenly disappear, and seemingly endless time may pass before the market recovers its lost ground and resumes the trend (if it *does* resume).

If only there were some way of profiting from each of those brief price swings along the way—selling near their peaks and buying near their lows—the frustrating reactions could be converted from a liability to an asset. Needless to say, the perfect timing necessary to accomplish this is a trader's dream that is never likely to be fully realized by anyone. However, the chart technician can employ certain techniques that will help him squeeze a profit out of many of those interim price swings.

A precaution to observe when planning such short-term "in-and-out" trading is to avoid selling short within an uptrend or buying long within a downtrend. It might also be advisable to hold some portion of one's position intact in the direction of the "trading trend" from start to finish, so as to avoid the possibility of missing part of the main move as a result of a "temporary" liquidation that could not be reinstated as planned.

The first requirement, of course, is to determine to one's satisfaction the main direction of the "trading trend." This can be accomplished by applying the trend techniques outlined in this book, by utilizing an automatic trend method that seems appropriate, or by using some combination of automatic techniques and general chart analysis.

One obvious characteristic of any extended price move is the tendency for price swings in the direction of the trend to be more extensive than the swings against the trend. It will also be found that the size of the short-term swings and counter-swings will often be related to the vertical width of the minor-trend curved channel as described in Chapter 4.

For example, let us say that we are trading Pork Bellies and have determined that the minor trend is moving within a curved channel 500 points wide. There will then be a tendency for many day-to-day price swings to trace about 500 points in the direction of the minor trend before reacting, and to react about 250 points against the trend. If the trend is shallow—that is, progressing at a slow pace—the swings in the direction of the trend are likely to be somewhat *smaller* than the 500-point channel width, and reactions are likely to be somewhat *larger* than half the channel width. If the trend is relatively steep, the main trend swings are likely to be *greater* than the channel width and reactions *less* than half the width during the steep climb.

If one is uncertain as to the correct vertical width of the channel in any commodity, he should test out a round figure equal to about 5% of the prevailing price level. It should then be determined whether most recent price swings in the direction of the minor trend closely match that number, or whether a larger or smaller figure might be more appropriate.

The size of the curved channel, however, should be used only as a starting point for estimating the probable extent of the swings and counterswings. Other confirming measurements should be sought, in accordance with the Rule of Multiple Techniques described in Chapter 1. For example, one should project various price objectives, utilizing support and resistance areas, Rule-of-Seven measurements, the 17–35 measurement, and the 50% reaction rule. The charts should be watched for signs of small "drift" patterns that might give added importance to a short-term price objective. Trendlines and Predicted Trendlines should be utilized. Also, if one is in a position to keep in close touch with market action during trading hours, the timing of a short-term trade might be helped by paying attention to gap openings when they occur.

If only a very small position is to be taken in each commodity, the buy and sell points must be determined with much caution; if a large position is taken, sales can be averaged on a scale up around one or more target prices, and purchases can be averaged on a scale down in the same way. This latter procedure would decrease the probability of completely missing a trade by overestimating the likely extent of the price swing ahead, and would improve results in the case of an underestimated swing objective.

While in-and-out trading of day-to-day swings can be partly mechanical in nature, it must be based mainly on the chartist's technical judgment of the market. The decision as to whether or not to use this type of trading will depend largely on the temperament of each individual trader, and how quickly he is able to respond to intra-day price fluctuations.

Volume and Open Interest

Up to now nothing has been said here about volume and open interest. There is no doubt that the relationship between the price trend in a futures market and the volume and open interest trends in that market can often give a clue to the future direction of that market. However, in my opinion, the analysis of volume and open interest should probably be considered one of the less important tools of the chart technician. The significance of volume and open interest has been thoroughly covered in an excellent booklet titled "Volume and Open Interest: A Key to Commodity Price Forecasting," published by the Commodity Research Bureau, Inc., New York.

Generally speaking, during bull trends there is a tendency for volume and open interest to expand during a price advance and to contract during a price decline. In a bear trend, the tendency is for volume and open interest to expand on dips and to contract on rallies. This normal tendency can be distorted or even reversed at times as a result of various influences. For one thing, many markets show a seasonal expansion and contraction of open interest, and that seasonal tendency must be taken into account. Secondly, both volume and open interest can be greatly distorted by straddles, which might account for a substantial portion of trading activity at times, and yet have no real bearing on the supply or demand of the commodity.

There is no doubt, however, that volume in particular can sometimes give a clue to the validity of a price movement. Good automatic trading methods have been devised that include volume and open interest in their computations. Care should be taken, however, to avoid any such plan that puts more emphasis on volume and open interest than on price movement. Any plan that permits a position to be held while the price moves persistently in the wrong direction could prove disastrous.

*   *   *

This completes the summing up of the bar-chart techniques described in this book. I hope that the reader will be able to utilize some of those techniques to his financial advantage. I hope, too, that the contents of this book will stimulate others to do further research into commodity price movements, and to discover new and even better techniques.

APPENDIX A

Table 1
Data for Figure 1—Random Walk—"Daily Closing Prices"

Week No.	Random No.	Simulated Price	Week No.	Random No.	Simulated Price	Week No.	Random No.	Simulated Price	Week No.	Random No.	Simulated Price
1		1000	6	−13	1014	11	− 6	1043	16	−35	1017
	−12	988		−48	966		−10	1033		−46	971
	+29	1017		+39	1005		−23	1010		−40	931
	− 5	1012		+26	1031		−18	992		−30	901
	−29	983		+23	1054		+47	1039		0	901
	−49	934									
2	+46	980	7	+49	1103	12	−17	1022	17	−32	869
	+45	1025		−31	1072		+30	1052		+15	884
	+44	1069		−30	1041		+39	1091		+49	933
	−18	1051		− 7	1035		+47	1138		+ 8	941
	− 2	1049		+38	1073		−20	1118		−10	931
3	−15	1034	8	+30	1043	13	−49	1069	18	− 3	928
	+11	1045		+39	1082		−48	1021		−45	883
	−45	1000		−19	1063		−11	1010		+50	933
	+ 7	1007		+39	1102		+35	1045		+41	974
	+23	1030		−27	1075		+22	1067		+18	992
4	+ 8	1038	9	+26	1101	14	−40	1027	19	−35	957
	−47	991		−10	1091		−40	987		0	957
	−18	973		+28	1119		+37	1024		+13	970
	+48	1021		−27	1092		+16	1040		−35	935
	+27	1048		− 2	1090		+27	1067		−33	902
5	+10	1058	10	−48	1042	15	+14	1081	20	+36	938
	−41	1017		−27	1015		+25	1106		+40	978
	+31	1048		+15	1030		−35	1071		+39	1017
	+22	1070		+25	1055		+27	1098		−40	977
	−43	1027		− 6	1049		−46	1052		−37	940

No.			No.			No.			No.		
21	+37	977	27	+32	936	33	−35	887	39	+43	753
	−15	962		− 6	930		− 3	884		−25	728
	−11	951		+49	979		− 8	876		−13	715
	+10	961		−13	966		− 6	870		−14	701
	−38	923		−25	941		−31	839		−29	672
22	− 4	919	28	−24	917	34	− 5	834	40	+40	712
	+ 7	926		−23	894		−47	787		+49	761
	−40	886		−21	873		+30	817		0	761
	− 3	883		−47	826		− 1	816		−21	740
	+36	919		−29	797		+50	866		−42	698
23	−43	876	29	+27	824	35	+25	891	41	+24	722
	−37	839		− 9	815		+43	934		+37	759
	+27	866		+25	840		−36	898		−42	717
	+48	914		−36	804		−48	850		+ 3	720
	+23	937		+50	854		−27	823		−27	693
24	−49	888	30	+41	895	36	+27	850	42	+35	728
	+ 3	891		+46	941		−18	832		+ 7	735
	−11	880		+35	976		+24	856		−43	692
	− 2	878		0	976		− 1	855		− 3	689
	− 4	874		+26	1002		−34	821		+28	717
25	−25	849	31	−24	978	37	+ 2	823	43	+12	729
	+19	868		+43	1021		− 1	822		−44	685
	+ 6	874		+46	1067		+ 7	829		−21	664
	+10	884		+ 2	1069		0	829		−50	614
	−13	871		−43	1026		−36	793		+31	645
26	+32	903	32	−36	990	38	− 7	786	44	−28	617
	+27	930		− 9	981		−33	753		−45	572
	−44	886		+21	1002		−42	711		+ 2	574
	−10	876		−45	957		+15	726		+18	592
	+28	904		−35	922		−16	710		−23	569

Table 1 (continued)
Data for Figure 1—Random Walk—"Daily Closing Prices"

Week No.	Random No.	Simu-lated Price	Week No.	Random No.	Simu-lated Price	Week No.	Random No.	Simu-lated Price	Week No.	Random No.	Simu-lated Price
45	+17	586	50	−21	549	55	+20	758	60	−27	458
	− 8	578		+11	560		−39	719		+46	504
	− 9	569		0	560		+31	750		− 1	503
	+29	598		+35	595		−18	732		−39	464
	−35	563		−17	578		−35	697		−22	442
46	+32	595	51	−13	565	56	+39	736	61	−32	410
	−17	578		−29	536		−15	721		+41	451
	−19	559		+10	546		+12	733		+12	463
	−46	513		−17	529		+ 6	739		+10	473
	−41	472		+13	542		+34	773		+24	497
47	−23	449	52	−34	508	57	− 5	768	62	+ 8	505
	+17	466		− 1	507		−39	729		+26	531
	+34	500		+26	533		−34	695		−32	499
	−48	452		+ 7	540		−43	652		+50	549
	−50	402		+ 5	545		−21	631		−50	499
48	+ 8	410	53	+49	594	58	+43	674	63	+22	521
	+34	444		+25	619		−43	631		+42	563
	+38	482		+17	636		−32	599		−32	531
	+ 9	491		−47	589		+16	615		− 9	522
	+38	529		+12	601		−47	568		−48	474
49	− 3	526	54	+40	641	59	−49	519	64	+ 7	481
	+45	571		+26	667		+48	567		−39	442
	−15	556		+22	689		−26	541		+10	452
	−21	535		+12	701		−36	505		+29	481
	+35	570		+37	738		−20	485		+22	503

65		67		69		71	
−16	487	+50	630	+27	857	−43	795
+32	519	+19	649	+37	894	0	795
+41	560	+10	659	−25	869	+32	827
+34	594	+27	686	−30	839	−27	800
+25	619	+21	707	+13	852	+44	844
66		68		70		72	
− 9	610	+ 1	708	−10	842	−25	819
+28	638	+42	750	+ 4	846	+10	829
−32	606	+48	798	−46	800	−38	791
−28	578	+25	823	−12	788	0	791
+ 2	580	+ 7	830	+50	838	−29	762

Table 2
Data for Figure 2—Random Walk—"Daily High, Low, Close"

Week No.	Random Numbers			Simulated Price		
	High	Low	Close	High	Low	Close
1	+1	−7	−6	101	93	94
	+5	−1	+4	99	93	98
	0	−6	−2	98	92	96
	+4	−5	−1	100	91	95
	+7	−8	+6	102	87	101
2	+1	−10	0	102	91	101
	+4	−7	−7	105	94	94
	+8	−8	−1	102	86	93
	+8	+3	+4	101	96	97
	+10	+2	+6	107	99	103
3	+8	−10	+5	111	93	108
	+10	−5	+9	118	103	117
	−6	−8	−7	111	109	110
	+6	−6	+2	116	104	112
	+8	−5	+4	120	107	116
4	+6	−9	−2	122	107	114
	0	−6	−5	114	108	109
	+7	0	+3	116	109	112
	+10	−9	+3	122	103	115
	−1	−5	−4	114	110	111
5	+4	−6	0	115	105	111
	+9	+4	+9	120	115	120
	+5	−10	−5	125	110	115
	+8	−1	+2	123	114	117
	+8	−10	−3	125	107	114
6	+7	−9	−2	121	105	112
	+7	−9	−1	119	103	111
	+7	−1	+3	118	110	114
	+7	−1	0	121	131	114
	+2	−9	−7	116	105	107
7	+3	−5	0	110	102	107
	+10	−2	+5	117	105	112
	+5	−9	−4	117	103	108
	+10	−10	+5	118	98	113
	+5	−6	0	118	107	113
8	+1	−9	−5	114	104	108
	0	−4	−3	108	104	105
	+6	−10	−6	111	95	99
	+7	0	+2	106	99	101
	+3	−7	+3	104	94	104
9	+10	−6	+9	114	98	113
	+1	−6	0	114	107	113
	+10	−6	+5	123	107	118
	+10	+1	+8	128	119	126
	−1	−8	−5	125	118	121
10	+9	+2	+8	130	123	129
	+9	−8	+6	138	121	135
	+10	−5	+8	145	130	143
	+4	−2	+3	147	141	146
	+9	0	+1	155	146	147

Table (groups 11–16):

Group						
11	152	137	141	−6	−10	+5
	142	134	136	−5	−7	+1
	145	134	136	0	−2	+9
	131	128	129	−7	−8	−5
	134	122	133	+4	−7	+5
12	137	123	131	−2	−10	+4
	134	128	133	+2	−3	+3
	130	124	127	−6	−9	−3
	135	127	134	+7	0	+8
	140	134	138	+4	0	+6
13	142	136	137	−1	−2	+4
	144	130	136	−1	−7	+7
	142	129	139	+3	−7	+6
	142	130	139	0	−9	+3
	144	131	143	+4	−8	+5
14	153	150	152	+9	+7	+10
	162	145	155	+3	−7	+10
	165	160	163	+8	+5	+10
	164	158	163	0	−5	+1
	169	153	160	−3	−10	+6
15	169	150	155	−5	−10	+9
	161	147	148	−7	−8	+6
	149	146	148	0	−2	+1
	144	141	143	−5	−7	−4
	151	134	146	+3	−9	+8
16	140	136	138	−8	−10	−6
	143	136	137	−1	−2	+5
	140	129	136	−1	−8	+3
	144	136	143	+7	0	+8
	135	134	135	−8	−9	−8

Table (groups 17–22):

Group						
17	132	126	141	−3	−9	+6
	139	122	141	+7	−10	+9
	140	134	147	+1	−5	+8
	140	132	148	0	−8	+8
	138	137	148	−2	−3	+8
18	141	138	142	+3	0	+4
	138	135	141	−3	−6	0
	144	129	147	+6	−9	+1
	145	134	145	+1	−10	+7
	146	139	152	+1	−6	+7
19	139	137	149	−7	−9	+3
	135	134	139	−4	−5	0
	132	127	142	−3	−8	+7
	138	130	140	+6	−2	+8
	131	128	137	−7	−10	−1
20	133	131	140	+2	0	+9
	135	126	136	+2	−7	+3
	137	129	140	+2	−6	+5
	132	127	139	+5	−10	+2
	137	130	138	+5	−2	+6
21	136	131	140	−1	−6	+3
	133	128	146	−3	−8	+10
	138	128	143	+5	−5	+10
	132	130	138	−6	−8	0
	126	125	132	−6	−7	0
22	124	123	136	−2	−3	+10
	116	114	133	−8	−10	+9
	116	111	119	0	−5	+3
	116	106	122	0	−10	+6
	116	115	116	0	−1	0

Table 2 (continued)
Data for Figure 2—Random Walk—"Daily High, Low, Close"

Week No.	Random Numbers High	Low	Close	Simulated Price High	Low	Close
23	+7	+1	+4	123	117	120
	+8	-10	+4	128	110	124
	+5	-3	+1	129	121	125
	+9	+1	+5	134	126	130
	+3	-9	0	133	121	130
24	-1	-8	-2	129	122	128
	+5	-1	+1	133	127	129
	-7	-10	-10	122	119	119
	+10	-6	+3	129	113	122
	+4	+1	+4	126	123	126
25	+7	-2	+5	133	124	131
	+10	-5	+6	141	126	137
	+10	+1	+7	147	136	144
	+5	0	0	149	144	144
	+1	-7	-6	145	137	138
26	0	-6	-4	138	132	134
	+8	-4	+5	142	130	139
	+5	0	+2	144	139	141
	+8	-2	+4	149	139	145
	+5	-2	+5	150	143	150
27	+7	-4	+5	157	146	155
	0	-4	-1	155	151	154
	+9	-9	-3	163	145	151
	+7	0	+6	158	151	157
	+6	0	+1	163	157	158
28	+10	-6	+5	168	152	163
	-2	-5	-3	161	158	160
	+9	-2	+1	169	158	161
	+5	0	0	166	161	161
	+6	-6	+1	167	155	162
29	+7	-8	+5	169	154	167
	+5	-4	-3	172	163	164
	+4	-8	+3	168	156	167
	+8	-5	0	175	162	167
	+3	-8	+3	170	159	170
30	+9	-5	+8	179	165	178
	+10	-3	-3	188	175	175
	+6	-8	0	181	167	175
	+3	+1	+2	178	176	177
	+8	-6	-6	185	171	171
31	+5	-10	+3	176	161	174
	+7	-8	+1	181	166	175
	+9	-1	+5	184	174	180
	+4	-3	-2	184	177	178
	0	-8	0	178	170	178
32	+10	-10	-1	188	168	177
	+2	-8	0	179	169	177
	+5	-1	0	182	176	177
	+10	-8	-4	187	169	173
	+10	-9	-4	183	164	169

39									
+8	−3	+4	194	183	190				
+10	−10	+7	200	180	183				
+8	−3	+5	191	180	188				
+9	−9	+4	197	179	184				
+3	−8	−3	187	176	181				

40					
+6	−10	−4	187	171	177
+6	−8	−1	183	169	176
+3	−4	0	179	172	176
+1	−9	−4	177	167	172
+8	−3	+3	180	169	175

41					
+9	−10	−9	184	165	166
+3	−5	−4	169	161	162
−1	−9	−5	161	153	157
0	−10	0	157	147	157
+2	−6	−2	159	151	155

42					
+6	−7	−2	161	148	153
+10	−6	+6	163	147	159
+4	−6	−4	163	153	155
−1	−8	−6	154	147	149
+6	+1	+1	155	150	150

43					
+9	+6	+9	159	156	159
+3	−9	−2	162	150	157
+10	−1	0	167	156	157
+10	−7	+7	167	150	158
+9	−2	+5	167	156	163

44					
+3	−6	−6	166	157	159
+9	0	+8	168	159	167
+9	−6	+6	176	161	173
0	−4	−1	173	169	172
+5	−8	−7	177	164	165

33					
+8	−8	−4	177	161	165
+4	−3	+2	169	162	167
+6	−2	+6	173	165	173
+10	+1	+4	183	174	177
+9	−2	+9	186	175	186

34					
0	−9	0	186	177	186
+6	−10	−9	192	176	177
+5	−10	−9	182	167	168
+7	+2	+7	175	170	175
+6	−9	−8	181	166	167

35					
+6	−7	−6	173	160	161
+7	−5	−1	168	156	160
+8	−7	+4	168	153	164
+10	−2	+4	174	162	168
0	−2	−1	168	166	167

36					
+3	0	0	170	167	167
+3	−6	+2	170	161	169
+6	−3	+3	175	166	172
−3	−9	−5	169	163	167
+6	−4	+1	173	163	168

37					
+7	−2	0	175	166	168
+6	−3	+5	174	165	173
+2	−2	−1	175	171	172
0	−8	−8	172	164	164
+5	0	+5	169	164	169

38					
+8	0	+7	177	169	176
+7	−5	−3	183	171	173
+9	−4	+6	182	169	179
+9	+3	+8	188	182	187
+5	−7	−1	192	180	186

Table 2 (continued)
Data for Figure 2—Random Walk—"Daily High, Low, Close"

Week No.	Random Numbers			Simulated Price			Week No.	Random Numbers			Simulated Price		
	High	Low	Close	High	Low	Close		High	Low	Close	High	Low	Close
45	+1	−8	−5	166	157	160	50	+4	−7	−6	159	148	149
	0	−10	−1	160	150	159		+4	0	+4	153	149	153
	+9	−7	+5	168	152	164		+9	+1	+5	162	154	158
	+2	−4	−1	166	160	163		+9	−10	−2	167	148	156
	+5	−9	−3	168	154	160		+4	+1	+3	160	157	159
46	+10	−9	0	170	151	160	51	+5	−6	+5	164	153	164
	0	−8	0	160	152	160		+5	−7	+1	169	157	165
	+6	0	+4	166	160	164		+6	−7	−1	171	158	164
	+2	−10	−8	166	154	156		+5	−10	+4	169	154	168
	+9	−10	+3	165	146	159		0	−7	−6	168	161	162
47	+7	−7	+6	166	152	165	52	0	−7	−2	162	155	160
	0	−6	−4	165	159	161		−4	−7	−6	156	153	154
	−1	−10	−1	160	151	160		+10	−10	−5	164	144	149
	+2	−4	−3	162	156	157		+1	−10	−1	150	139	148
	−1	−6	−2	156	151	155		+6	−1	+3	154	147	151
48	+9	+1	+8	164	156	163	53	−3	−9	−9	148	142	142
	+4	−5	−3	167	158	160		+10	+6	+9	152	148	151
	+5	−2	+3	165	158	163		+10	−10	−6	161	141	145
	+9	−6	+5	172	157	168		+8	−3	0	153	142	145
	+8	−1	0	176	167	168		+10	+1	+7	155	146	152
49	+4	−9	+2	172	159	170							
	+6	−2	−1	176	168	169							
	+1	−5	−1	170	164	168							
	−4	−6	−5	164	162	163							
	+8	−10	−8	171	153	155							

APPENDIX **B**

Simplified Method for Calculating Linear Least-Squares Trendlines

The chartist who wishes to experiment with linear least squares trendlines will find it helpful to use an electronic calculator that has been preprogrammed for that work rather than go through the chore of calculating each separate step of the formula. On the calculator he simply sums up the prices in the series and presses the appropriate keys to quickly obtain the value (y) of the least squares trendline on any day (x). Nevertheless, he should know how to do the calculations without the help of sophisticated equipment if the need should arise. Machines sometimes have a way of breaking down at the most inopportune times.

The purpose of this section is to provide the reader with a relatively simple method for finding the points on a linear least squares trendline of reasonable length without the necessity of solving all the equations in the process. The results obtained by this simple method will be identical to those obtained by the standard procedure. The key difference between the two methods is that in the simpler method to be described here the linear least squares trendline has its point of origin at the center of the time series instead of at the beginning of the series. The value at that central point will always be the simple arithmetic average of the prices in the series. Once the slope of the line is determined it is a simple matter to extend the line in both directions from the center.

In the explanation that follows we will always refer to the time series in terms of a certain number of "days." However, if it serves the chartist's purpose, he can substitute "weeks" for "days," using weekly prices instead of daily prices, or he could substitute "months" or even "years" if he wishes.

The equation for a linear least squares trendline is

$$y = a + bx$$

In this equation "y" is the price level of the least squares trendline on any day "x." In the simplified method described here, "a" is simply the arithmetic mean (average price) of the price series. It is obtained by adding the prices in the series and dividing the sum by the number of prices in the series. The letter "b" is the slope of the line, or the amount the line moves up or down each day. The days "x" are numbered consecutively starting with zero at the midpoint and counting forwards with plus signs and backwards with minus signs.

In a five-day price series the "x" values for each day are as follows:

Day No.	"x" Value
1	−2
2	−1
3	0
4	+1
5	+2

To obtain the value of "b" (the slope of the line) there are three steps necessary. In a five-day price series the three steps are as follows:

1) Take the price on each day of the series and multiply that price by its corresponding "x" value. (In a five-day series the third day will always multiply out to zero.)
2) Sum up the values obtained in step one above.
3) Divide the sum by 10 (in a five-day series only).
   The result is the value of "b."

To demonstrate the complete procedure for obtaining the points of a five-day least-squares trendline, let us take a simple series of prices such as 5, 7, 12, 11, 15. The calculations are as follows:

Day No.	Price	"x"	Product of Price and "x"
1	5	−2	−10
2	7	−1	− 7
3	12	0	0
4	11	+1	+11
5	15	+2	+30

Sum: 50   +24
Solution: a = 50 ÷ 5 = 10
           b = 24 ÷ 10 = 2.4
    Since y = a + bx
           y =10 + 2.4 (x)

The least squares trendline for the above series of five prices starts at a price level of 10 on the third day and slopes up and down at the rate of 2.4 per day.

The value of "y" on each day can be figured as follows:

$$\text{"y" on day \#1 is } 10 - 4.8 = 5.2$$
$$\text{"y" on day \#2 is } 10 - 2.4 = 7.6$$
$$\text{"y" on day \#3 is } 10 + \ \ 0 = 10.0$$
$$\text{"y" on day \#4 is } 10 + 2.4 = 12.4$$
$$\text{"y" on day \#5 is } 10 + 4.8 = 14.8$$

In the above series we can go a step further and project the "y" value of the least squares trendline to the sixth day or any later day, since the line advances at a regular rate of 2.4 per day.

When the price series consists of an odd number of prices, such as in the five-day price series just described, the center of the series always coincides with an actual price. A complication arises when there are an even number of prices in the series, since the center of the series will be between the two middle prices. This problem can be overcome by assigning "x" values of −0.5 and +0.5 to the two central days of the series. (This will not affect the value of "a," which will always be the arithmetic average of the prices in the series.) In a 10-day series, for example, the "x" values of days one through 10 would be −4.5, −3.5, −2.5, −1.5, −0.5, +0.5, +1.5, +2.5, +3.5, +4.5.

Regardless of how many days there are in the price series the slope "b" is always obtained in three steps: (1) multiply the price on each day by its corresponding "x" value; 2) sum up those products; and 3) divide that sum by a certain number that is different for each length of series. As already indicated, that divisor in a five-day series is 10. However, it increases progressively for each larger series. Following is a list of the divisors to be used in any series from three to 25 prices:

Days in series	Divisor for "b"	Days in series	Divisor for "b"
3	2	14	227.5
4	5	15	280
5	10	16	340
6	17.5	17	408
7	28	18	484.5
8	42	19	570
9	60	20	665
10	82.5	21	770
11	110	22	885.5
12	143	23	1012
13	182	24	1150
		25	1300

Armed with the above formulas and an ordinary hand calculator, the chartist should be able to plot a linear least squares trendline, or find its value on any selected day, in any series containing up to 25 prices.

Weighted Average Method

For commodity traders the most useful points on a least squares trendline are probably the values on the last day of the series (today), on the following day (tomorrow) and perhaps at the point of origin (the first day). Any one of those three values can be obtained in a single step by simply using a specially weighted average for the series. In Chapter 4 (Curved Trend Channels) we gave the weighted average formula for projecting a 5-day series of prices to the 5th day, and the formula for projecting a 3-week series to the 3rd week. Those figures are included in the tabulation of "Weighted Average Equivalents" listed here. The weights for each series from 3 to

WEIGHTED AVERAGE EQUIVALENT OF LEAST SQUARES TRENDLINE
Multiply the price on each day of the series by its corresponding
weight. The sum of the products equals the projected value of the
Least Squares Trendline to the day indicated.

3 DAY SERIES

To Day #3 Day / Weight	To Day #4 Day / Weight
1 -.166667	1 -.666667
2 +.333333	2 +.333333
3 +.833333	3 +1.33333

4 DAY SERIES

To Day #4 Day / Weight	To Day #5 Day / Weight
1 -.2	1 -.5
2 +.1	2 0 zero
3 +.4	3 +.5
4 +.7	4 +1.

5 DAY SERIES

To Day #5 Day / Weight	To Day #6 Day / Weight
1 -.2	1 -.4
2 0 zero	2 -.1
3 +.2	3 +.2
4 +.4	4 +.5
5 +.6	5 +.8

6 DAY SERIES

To Day #6 Day / Weight	To Day #7 Day / Weight
1 -.190476	1 -.333333
2 -.047619	2 -.133333
3 +.095238	3 +.066667
4 +.238095	4 +.266667
5 +.380952	5 +.466667
6 +.523810	6 +.666667

7 DAY SERIES

To Day #7 Day / Weight	To Day #8 Day / Weight
1 -.178571	1 -.285714
2 -.071429	2 -.142857
3 +.035714	3 0 zero
4 +.142857	4 +.142857
5 +.25	5 +.285714
6 +.357143	6 +.428571
7 +.464286	7 +.571429

8 DAY SERIES

To Day #8 Day / Weight	To Day #9 Day / Weight
1 -.166667	1 -.25
2 -.083333	2 -.142857
3 0 zero	3 -.035714
4 +.083333	4 +.071429
5 +.166667	5 +.178571
6 +.25	6 +.285714
7 +.333333	7 +.392857
8 +.416667	8 +.5

9 DAY SERIES

To Day #9 Day / Weight	To Day #10 Day / Weight
1 -.155556	1 -.222222
2 -.088889	2 -.138889
3 -.022222	3 -.055556
4 +.044444	4 +.027778
5 +.111111	5 +.111111
6 +.177778	6 +.194444
7 +.244444	7 +.277778
8 +.311111	8 +.361111
9 +.377778	9 +.444444

10 DAY SERIES

To Day #10 Day / Weight	To Day #11 Day / Weight
1 -.145455	1 -.2
2 -.090909	2 -.133333
3 -.036364	3 -.066667
4 +.018182	4 0 zero
5 +.072727	5 +.066667
6 +.127273	6 +.133333
7 +.181818	7 +.2
8 +.236364	8 +.266667
9 +.290909	9 +.333333
10 +.345455	10 +.4

11 DAY SERIES

To Day #11 Day / Weight	To Day #12 Day / Weight
1 -.136364	1 -.181818
2 -.090909	2 -.127274
3 -.045455	3 -.072727
4 0 zero	4 -.018182
5 +.045455	5 +.036364
6 +.090909	6 +.090909
7 +.136364	7 +.145455
8 +.181818	8 +.2
9 +.227273	9 +.254545
10 +.272727	10 +.309091
11 +.318182	11 +.363636

12 DAY SERIES

To Day #12 Day / Weight	To Day #13 Day / Weight
1 -.128205	1 -.166667
2 -.089744	2 -.121212
3 -.051282	3 -.075758
4 -.012821	4 -.030303
5 +.025641	5 +.015152
6 +.064103	6 +.060606
7 +.102564	7 +.106061
8 +.141026	8 +.151515
9 +.179487	9 +.196970
10 +.217949	10 +.242424
11 +.256410	11 +.287879
12 +.294872	12 +.333333

13 DAY SERIES

To Day #13 Day / Weight	To Day #14 Day / Weight
1 -.120879	1 -.153846
2 -.087912	2 -.115385
3 -.054945	3 -.076923
4 -.021979	4 -.038462
5 +.010989	5 0 zero
6 +.043956	6 +.038462
7 +.076923	7 +.076923
8 +.109890	8 +.115385
9 +.142857	9 +.153846
10 +.175824	10 +.192308
11 +.208791	11 +.230769
12 +.241758	12 +.269231
13 +.274725	13 +.307692

14 DAY SERIES

To Day #14 Day / Weight	To Day #15 Day / Weight
1 -.114286	1 -.142857
2 -.085714	2 -.109890
3 -.057143	3 -.076923
4 -.028571	4 -.043956
5 0 zero	5 -.010989
6 +.028571	6 +.021978
7 +.057143	7 +.054945
8 +.085714	8 +.087912
9 +.114286	9 +.120879
10 +.142857	10 +.153846
11 +.171429	11 +.186813
12 +.2	12 +.219780
13 +.228571	13 +.252747
14 +.257143	14 +.285714

15 DAY SERIES

To Day #15 Day / Weight	To Day #16 Day / Weight
1 -.108333	1 -.133333
2 -.083333	2 -.104762
3 -.058333	3 -.076190
4 -.033333	4 -.047619
5 -.008333	5 -.019048
6 +.016667	6 +.009524
7 +.041667	7 +.038095
8 +.066667	8 +.066667
9 +.091667	9 +.095238
10 +.116667	10 +.123810
11 +.141667	11 +.152381
12 +.166667	12 +.180952
13 +.191667	13 +.209524
14 +.216667	14 +.238096
15 +.241667	15 +.266667

15 days (or weeks) are listed. Most of the weights are endless decimals that have been carried out to six decimal places. In actual practice four decimal places will give an accurate enough answer for
trading purposes, and you might even get by with two decimal
places. To obtain the value at day #1 you use the same weights as
those used for projecting to the last day of the series (first column),
but in *reverse* order. The answers obtained with the simple use of
these weighted averages will be identical to those that would be
obtained through the more complex calculation of $y = a + bx$.

Index

About the Author

Arthur Sklarew's involvement with commodities started in the early 1930s when he was a commission broker and import agent in the cash coffee market in New York. It was then that he first began to use price charts and moving averages in advising customers on the timing of their purchases and sales. In the late 1940s he expanded into cocoa importing, and in 1950 acquired a membership on the New York Cocoa Exchange. When he eventually realized that he was making far more money in futures than in his cash business, he decided to concentrate on the former exclusively. Since 1963 he has been associated with a major Wall Street commission house.

He was an avid student of market technical phenomena for those same years, constantly experimenting with new approaches, techniques, and methods. (He earned his reading glasses, he said, peering at price charts.) This, his first book, is the distillate of more than three decades of experimentation and inquiry into the price behavior of commodity markets.

www.ingramcontent.com/pod-product-compliance
Lightning Source LLC
Chambersburg PA
CBHW032329210326
41518CB00041B/1984